NEW YORK POST

Déjà Blue

THE NEW YORK GIANTS' 2011 CHAMPIONSHIP SEASON

Giants coach Tom Coughlin happily hands the Lombardi Trophy to Super Bowl XLVI MVP Eli Manning after Big Blue defeated the Patriots 21-17 in Indianapolis. It was the second Super Bowl win for both. (Rob Carr/Getty Images)

This book is available in quantity at special discounts for your group or organization.
For further information, contact:

Triumph Books LLC
542 South Dearborn Street
Suite 750
Chicago, IL 60605
Phone: (312) 939-3330
Fax: (312) 663-3557

www.triumphbooks.com

Printed in U.S.A.
ISBN: 978-1-60078-744-7

Content packaged by Mojo Media, Inc.
Joe Funk: Editor
Jason Hinman: Creative Director

Front and back cover photos by N.Y. Post: Charles Wenzelberg

CONTENTS

INTRODUCTION

By Mike Vaccaro

It's really never like the movies, is it? No matter how much Hollywood sprinkles itself into real life, you really never get one defining moment, one turning point, one instant when you know — you just know — that the good guys are going to win, that the hero's going to get the girl, that the villain — or multiple villains — are going to get theirs.

No, real life unfolds in a more haphazard, more random way. A moment here, a moment there, and before you know it you're riding a wave, not at all certain where it's leading you or when it's going to end. And that's the best part really.

Because sometimes it never ends.

Sometimes, as the 2011 New York Giants proved, the very best of these journeys occurs when you can't possibly know they're coming.

"I can't say we didn't think about winning a championship because that's your goal every year, it's why you compete, it's why you get into this business in the first place," said Jerry Reese, the Giants' general manager, the man who not only selected the men who comprised a world championship roster, but also the man who had to find replacements and reinforcements on the fly when defections and injuries threatened to split the ground under the team's spikes.

"But I will say this," Reese said. "A season like this, when you are struggling, you say to yourself, 'OK. Let's just start winning games again.' And the it's 'OK, let's get in the playoffs, take out chances.' And then you get in, you say, 'You know what? Let's win a game or two, see if we can make a run.'"

He smiled.

"And then when you actually make that kind of a run...."

Reese knows where all of this starts, back in August, when every day seemed to bring a new calamity. Tight end Kevin Boss signed with the Raiders. Receiver Steve Smith left for the Eagles. An old Super Bowl hero fallen on hard times, Plaxico Burress, was released from prison, paid a cursory visit to the Giants' training facilities, then promptly signed across town with the Jets.

Every day, it seemed, radio airwaves were littered with anxious Giants fans wondering if Reese was aware that the lockout had ended. Every night, inboxes would be stuffed with speculation that Reese — who'd only won a Super Bowl his first try out of the box who was already the Giants GM with the highest career winning percentage. The Eagles and Jets, two bitter rivals, were making news every day. The Giants were awfully quiet.

"Talk to me," John Mara, the team's co-owner, said one day during training camp, "when we've played a few games with the players we do have."

The problem was, once the games began, the news got even worse. Every day during the exhibition, it seemed, the Giants were dealt devastating blows, starting with Terrell Thomas, a fourth-year cornerback who was expected to take a huge leap up in class, who blew out his knee against the Bears in the preseason. He was followed, in ridiculously rapid fashion, by Jonathan Goff, the middle linebacker who tore an ACL before the season opener in Washington; linebacker Clint Sintim, another ACL tear; Marvin Austin, Brian Witherspoon, Bruce Johnson — the list went on forever.

Then Osi Umenyiora got hurt. He missed time. So did Justin Tuck. So did No. 1 pick Prince Amukamara. It was like a plague had hit the Giants.

But a funny thing happened amid all this triage.

Tom Coughlin — and not for the last time — gathered his team and delivered a simple message.

"I believe in this team," he told them before the opener. "I believe in the players who are here. I feel badly for the players who aren't here, because this is their livelihood. But I think we have plenty of football players in this room that can win a lot of games this year."

To the press, he made an additional point that, at the time, seemed a bit pie-eyed, laced with wishful thinking.

"I don't imagine you remember how many injuries the Packers suffered last year, do you?" he asked, smiling.

The answer was this: plenty, more than teams are supposed to bear, and yet the Packers got hot at exactly the right moment, they duplicated the Giants' trick of winning three road games in the NFC playoffs and then dispatched the Steelers in the Super Bowl, all the while carrying an injured reserved list that read like the Green Bay phone book.

The message was clear: the Packers didn't pack up the season when they started to run low on bandages and gauze.

So why would we?

It was a little under three months later when Coughlin would again gather his team together and offer a similar sliver of hope. This was in the aftermath of an ugly 49-24 crunching at New Orleans on Nov. 28. The Giants, who'd started 6-2, were now 6-5, and they'd lose the next week at home to Green Bay to go 6-6. They looked like a team in free-fall. Coughlin, whose job security was about as tenuous as a guy with a Super Bowl on his resume could possibly be, was shaking off another round of whispers and rumors.

And his football team was playing brutally.

The Coughlin of Jacksonville, the Coughlin of Boston College — and probably even the Coughlin of his early years with the Giants — would have shown the crisis on his face, would have relayed it with every public utterance. That was who he used to be, and even he would admit as much. But the Coughlin of 2011 was confident in his status and his stature, he had a Super Bowl ring as proof that his way worked. And there was something else.

"I know you want me to say that the sky is falling," he said. "But it isn't falling. This is a good team. We know we're good. We know we can win games. It's just a matter of doing it."

All coaches, in desperate straits, try to make their lot sound rosier than it is. And most of those coaches realize it is a desperate attempt to paint some acrylic over a crumbling wall. Only there was a different way about this. Coughlin didn't just say the words, it was clear he meant them. Even at 6-6. Even at 7-7, after losing a second game to the woeful Redskins.

Which made his optimism after season-savings wins over the Jets and Cowboys that much easier to understand. Which gave his energetic approval of the Giants' opening-round thrashing of the Falcons that much more credibility. And which made this magic-spackled dream ride all the more remarkable to observe as it wound its way through Green Bay, San Francisco and, at last, Indianapolis.

In the joyous aftermath of Giants 21, Patriots 17 on Feb. 5, Mara said, "There isn't another coach on earth I'd rather have than Tom Coughlin," but it didn't take Coughlin to expand the thought exponentially: "There isn't a team I'd rather have or players I'd rather coach," he said. "When you see a team come together, that's about as good as it gets in our game. And watching what these guys did ... heck, it just makes me smile to think about it."

A moment here. A moment there.

And before you know it, a wave.

A wave that sometimes doesn't stop until it's delivered you to the final stop on the line, the best stop in sports. The top of the world. Buckle up and strap in: we're recreating that trip every wonderful step of the way. Enjoy. ■

SUPER BOWL XLVI

FEBRUARY 5, 2012 | GIANTS 21, PATRIOTS 17

ELITE REPEAT

Giants upset Patriots again for franchise's fourth title

By Paul Schwartz

At the end, Tom Coughlin did not need to push and prod his Giants, did not need to preach All In any longer, did not need to insist and demand and plea for his players to please, please, just Finish.

All he needed to do was watch the confetti fall after his quarterback, Eli Manning, did it again and Justin Tuck and his defense did it again, did it to Bill Belichick and Tom Brady again, incredibly, impossibly and, in some strange way, naturally.

"This is the finish line for this year, yes it is!" Coughlin exclaimed.

"I don't know if I could have written a better script than this one," Tuck said, beaming.

It is rare indeed when the perfect script becomes an even better story, but with these Giants, rare is where it's at. The Giants last night came back to beat the Patriots 21-17 in Super Bowl XLVI inside Lucas Oil Stadium in a classic game that actually equaled the 17-14 Giants victory over the Pats four years ago — a game that went down as perhaps the greatest Super Bowl ever played. Move over, Super Bowl XLII, there's a challenger for the throne, but there's no debate that Eli Manning sits atop it.

Just as he did four years, ago, Manning put his team on his back. This time, trailing 17-15, he drove the Giants 88 yards, channeling his magic David Tyree moment with a brilliant 38-yard pass to Mario Manningham, who tip-toed the left sideline between safeties Sterling Moore and Patrick Chung and made an epic catch that survived a replay challenge.

"I was in, man. It was a perfect, perfect pass," Manningham said.

The catch eventually led to Ahmad Bradshaw's 6-yard touchdown run with just 57 seconds left on a play where Bradshaw actually didn't want to score, as the Patriots were giving him a clear path and Manning — with the Giants already in chip-shot field goal range — was screaming "Fall down, fall down." Bradshaw stopped on the one-yard line but his momentum carried him into the end zone to make it 21-17.

"This is twice now we've been on the biggest stage and gone down the field and scored a touchdown when needed," guard Chris Snee said. "It all starts with Eli. He's tremendous in the huddle, tremendous in that situation, he just did a phenomenal job."

The Patriots got the ball back at their 20 with 57 seconds left and one timeout to work with.

Eli Manning rushes onto the field after the Patriots failed to score on the final play of Super Bowl XLVI. Moments earlier, Manning led the Giants downfield to score the game-winning touchdown. (N.Y. Post: Charles Wenzelberg)

Osi Umenyiora and Devin Thomas (right) celebrate after the Giants' dramatic Super Bowl win over the Patriots in Indy. (Rob Carr/Getty Images)

"In Foxborough (in a Nov. 6 24-20 victory over the Patriots) they scored what looked like a game winning drive and we were sick to our stomach," Tuck said. "I told the guys if they score here you're gonna be 25 times more sick to your stomach. A lot of guys lit up. We had to go out and finish, this is what we were built for, this I what we've been working for all year, we got 57 seconds to be world champions.

"It's just fitting it came down to a final drive by Eli and a closing out by our defense."

Fitting, and familiar, as that was the exact scenario that played out four years ago in Glendale, Ariz. Brady managed to throw for two first downs but he ran out of time, as his last-gasp Hail Mary in the end zone intended for Aaron Hernandez was knocked down in the end zone by Kenny Phillips to send the Giants into a euphoric celebration.

Manning, now a two-time MVP, completed 30 of 40 passes for 296 times, a first-quarter touchdown pass to Victor Cruz and, once again, no turnovers.

"This isn't about one person," Manning said. "This is about a team coming together, getting this win. I'm just proud of our guys, proud of this team and how we fought all year."

This journey to the promised land for the Giants was long and winding, as after 14 games the Giants were 7-7 and in put-up-or-shut-up mode, turning elimination into an every-week threat to their system. They haven't lost since, turning a high-wire act into an art form.

"This is just as exciting (as four years ago), probably more so, because of the kind

Victor Cruz grabs a 2-yard touchdown pass from Eli Manning as the Giants took an early 9-0 lead. (N.Y. Post: Charles Wenzelberg)

Mario Manningham hauls in a 38-yard Eli Manning pass and manages to land inbounds in the fourth quarter. He was initially ruled out of bounds, but the call was reversed on review. Manningham's catch was the key play on the Giants' game-winning scoring drive. (N.Y. Post: Charles Wenzelberg)

of year we had," Coughlin said. "What a wonderful experience it was to see this team come together like it did."

The Giants started with a flourish, getting a safety against Brady on the first Patriots play and Cruz' scoring grab to lead 9-0. The Patriots drove 96 yards to pull ahead 10-9 at halftime and 17-9 early in the third quarter as a torrid Brady completed a Super Bowl record 16 consecutive passes. Two Lawrence Tynes field goals closed the deficit to 17-15 after three quarters.

At the start of the fourth quarter, Brady somehow eluded a sack attempt by Linval Joseph, rolled right and fired deep downfield as Jason Pierre-Paul shoved him down. Chase Blackburn, in coverage against a clearly-laboring Rob Gronkowski, leaped and came up with an interception on the Giants 8-yard line. The Giants later caught a break when a wide-open Wes Welker couldn't hang on to a slightly high pass that Welker almost always catches, forcing a punt and giving Manning the ball for the winning drive.

Hard to believe.

"That's one thing we do well around here, believe," Tuck said. "You ain't got to pinch me. We all envisioned it kind of going this way, we all envisioned it going down to the fourth quarter. It's like Eli's driving, Manningham makes the catch, Bradshaw drives up the middle, it was almost relaxing, as crazy as that sounds. I'm sitting on the sideline smiling, just like, 'We've seen this before.'" ▪

Ahmad Bradshaw's "accidental" touchdown with a minute to go — scored when the Pats purposely left him untouched to get the ball back with time on the clock — will go down as one of the strangest plays in Super Bowl history. Bizarre, yes, but the running back's squatting, buckward fall into the end zone proved the game winner for the Giants. (N.Y. Post: Charles Wenzelberg)

New York's talented defensive line kept Tom Brady under pressure all night. Twice in the first half, the athletic Jason Pierre-Paul knocked down Brady passes at the line of scrimmage. (N.Y. Post: Charles Wenzelberg)

18

MANNING CANTON BOUND WITH SUPER SUPPORT SYSTEM

BY STEVE SERBY

When Eli Manning had done it again, beaten Tom Brady again in the last minute, his wife, Abby, handed him a gift far greater than his latest Super Bowl MVP trophy, handed him the little 10-month-old girl who couldn't take the keys to Manning's new black Corvette out of her mouth.

Eli Manning said to Ava Manning, "You got a new car, all right!" and kissed her on the cheek and began walking and carrying her through the bowels of Lucas Oil Stadium, and into the history books, toward Canton.

Elite Eli Manning, a 21-17 victor, the Greatest Quarterback in New York history.

This time he didn't have David Tyree when he took the ball at his 12 yard-line with 3:46 and one timeout left.

This time he had Mario Manningham.

Manning threw a perfect missile down the left sideline and hit Manningham, streaking past Sterling Moore, in stride, and Manningham, about to get belted out of bounds by Patrick Chung, managed to keep both feet in bounds in Toomer-esque fashion, and Manningham was at the 50, and nothing was going to stop Manning now.

And he knew it.

His teammates knew it.

Maybe Brady and Bill Belichick knew it.

Now Manning-to-Manningham again, for 16. Manning to D.J. Ware for 14. Finally, Ahmad Bradshaw was in the end zone, even though he tried to fall down at the 1 so Brady wouldn't have 57 seconds left.

"It [was] nervewracking," Manning said.

Brady tried a Hail Mary in the end zone for Aaron Hernandez and a crowd of Giants defenders left Gisele's prayers unanswered.

"This isn't about one person," Manning said. "This is about a whole team coming together, getting this win."

He was asked about his summer elite proclamation and said: "Y'all can debate that all you want. I just know we're world champions tonight, and that's what I'm most proud of."

Tyree, in a locker room every bit as euphoric as the one he remembers after Super Bowl XLII, began talking about the resolve Manningham showed after missing an earlier opportunity and the quarterback who threw him that miracle Catch 42.

"Honestly, every time I see Eli in a position where it's a two-minute drill, he has to win the game, I'm excited," Tyree said. "I think he's the best two-minute — even though it was a little longer than two minutes — but I think he's the best two-minute quarterback in football."

Ann Mara, the late Wellington Mara's widow, mother of Giants' co-owner John Mara, sat beaming in the middle of the Giants locker room.

"Eli Manning, he's definitely No. 1," Mrs. Mara said. "Definitely No. 1."

She was asked what she was thinking when her baby quarterback had the ball at the end with the Lombardi Trophy on the line, and she talked about her rosary beads.

"I asked the Blessed Mother to tell him where to throw the ball!" she said, laughing out loud, and added: "And she did!"

Eli Manning now has two Super Bowl MVPs to his credit, but the latest is richly deserved. The award caps a spectacular season by the 30-year-old quarterback, one in which he assumed the role of team leader and never faltered in guiding the Giants to the franchise's fourth Lombardi Trophy. (N.Y. Post: Charles Wenzelberg)

Down the hallway, Eli's mother talked about her boy with the ball at the end with the Lombardi Trophy on the line.

"I felt good about that," Olivia Manning said. "I believe in him, I really do. I believe in him. He's done it before. "

She had not yet seen Eli, but had blown him a kiss from afar.

"Eli's always been just really laid back and easy and guess what? He's got a little baby girl that's just like him."

The proud mom looked behind her to the carriage where Ava was resting.

"She also didn't want to miss the party, she's been up all this time clapping her hands and saying, 'Dada,'" Olivia said, and smiled.

Peyton Manning had watched it all from a different suite.

"This is sort of how we did it four years ago, and Peyton's kinda superstitious about things so he probably wanted to do the same thing again," Olivia said.

I asked Archie Manning what was going on inside him when his baby quarterback had the ball at the end with the Lombardi Trophy on the line.

"Well, I said, 'Here we go,'" Archie said.

I asked him what it is about Eli that enables him to thrive in those situations.

"He don't worry about too much," Archie said. "I think he just kinda bears down on what's in front of him."

Archie was reminded that Peyton had predicted Eli would win multiple Super Bowls.

"Peyton doesn't B.S. a lot.... There's nobody prouder tonight than Peyton, I can tell you that," Archie said.

Now Archie and John Mara embraced, and Mara gushed about Archie's boy.

"He just is so cool under pressure, he just doesn't get nervous, he doesn't get flustered.... There are not that many people on the planet that have that kind of DNA," Mara said.

Big brother Cooper Manning: "He's a calm, cool cat."

He's SuperMann II. ∎

Above: Giants fans celebrate in the Lucas Oil Stadium stands. Opposite: Manning was calm, efficient, and faultless under pressure against the Patriots. The Pats' D negated Victor Cruz and the long-passing game, but the quarterback moved the ball by hitting a variety of receivers with short- and midrange throws. (N.Y. Post: Charles Wenzelberg)

PREASEASON

BIG BLACK & BLUE

After Offseason to Forget, Kickoff Couldn't Come Soon Enough

By Mike Vaccaro

This isn't just the usual renewal Opening Day brings, any time, any sport, any season. Yes, there is something magical about snapping open this newspaper and seeing standings where all 32 teams sit on the same precise ledge, sporting identical 0-0 records.

Never does the impossible seem more possible than on Opening Day.

Never does boundless optimism of the true believer ring louder.

That applies to everyone, from Baltimore to Buffalo, from Seattle to St. Louis, from Denver to Dallas to Detroit. But nowhere does the flush and the rush of a real game come as more of a welcome island than for the Giants, who will take to the turf at FedEx Field amid a patriotic rush of a 9/11 ceremony, then take on the Redskins in a game that counts, blessedly, mercifully, for real.

"It's exciting, because there's been so much talk and so much anticipation and we really want to get started with the season," quarterback Eli Manning said earlier in the week. "There's a lot of talent in this room and I can't wait to see what it looks like once the season begins and everything counts for real."

The Giants endured one of the longest offseasons imaginable, one that really began in the fourth quarter of that horrific meltdown against the Eagles last December, one that endured a lockout, an endless string of defections early in training camp and a troubling rush of injuries late.

They enter this season where they exited last season, at this sprawling suburban mall of a stadium against a team that once upon a time was one of their most bitter rivals. When they were here last, on the day after New Year's, they tried their best to hang onto their 2010 season, beating the Redskins, while watching helplessly as the out-of-town scoreboard kept getting more and more grim, the Packers beating the Bears in Green Bay and putting an official lid on the Giants' collapse.

A few minutes later, John Mara gave a vote of confidence to the head coach, a vote that was backed up by a contract extension for Tom Coughlin last month. And for all the losses, Coughlin has remained a staunch believer these 2011 Giants have the goods to compete for the NFC East. Up and down the locker room, you hear the same thing.

"Everyone wants to draw conclusions before we even play games," defensive end Justin Tuck said. "But the only things that matter are the games. We'll see what happens then."

"This is football," running back Brandon Jacobs said. "This isn't a talk show."

Giants head coach Tom Coughlin looks on as the Giants stretch during their September 8 practice. (N.Y. Post: Charles Wenzelberg)

"I'm eager to see what we have, I think we all are," offensive coordinator Kevin Gilbride said. "I'm an anxious sort to begin with, but I really am anxious for this to start so we can see where we are for real."

That's the prevailing sentiment. That's what's sustained the Giants during a most unpredictable stretch bridging January and September, the soiled dreams of 2010 and the nascent ones of 2011. The Giants heard all about the losses, about receiver Steve Smith and tight end Kevin Boss, and they've sure heard a thing or two about Plaxico Burress.

They've seen the Jets bogart so many of the headlines locally, and the Eagles do the same within their division, adding players the way baseball card collectors gather doubles and triples rookie cards.

They've heard even their own fans — the staunchest and most loyal in town — mutter and groan and wring their hands and wrestle with doubt.

And now they get to play the games, games that count, games that get to define them for what they are — and what they aren't — separate and apart from speculation and skepticism.

"We're ready," Jacobs said.

That's good. It's time. ∎

Above: Running back Brandon Jacobs carries the ball during the Giants' August 16 practice. Opposite: Eli Manning throws a pass during the Giants training camp in East Rutherford, New Jersey. (N.Y. Post: Charles Wenzelberg)

REGULAR SEASON

SEPTEMBER 11, 2011 | REDSKINS 28, GIANTS 14

WHITE AND BLUES

Giants Call Anniversary Loss "Embarrassing"

By Paul Schwartz

They lost more than a game.

The record will show the Giants yesterday spent three hours doing very little to excite anyone about their prospects for this season and as a result fell, hard, to the Redskins, 28-14, in the opener at FedEx Field.

Even worse, though, a player who was designated as the defensive captain for the game believes the Giants let more than themselves down on the 10th anniversary of the Sept. 11 terrorist attacks.

"We came down here to get a win on a very important day for this football team, a very important day for the New York metropolitan area and we did not get the job done," defensive tackle Chris Canty said, his voice choked with passion.

"We don't live in a bubble as professional athletes. We're affected by what happens, we know what 9/11 means to us, what it means to our fans, what it means to our city, what it means to this country. We represent the red, white and blue and to go out there and put that kind of performance out there is just unacceptable for us.

"For us, understanding what we were representing today and to do what we did out there today, it's embarrassing."

By the time he was finished, Canty's eyes were moist.

Canty filled in for inactive Justin Tuck as a game captain and his defense could not get off the field often enough, could not solve

the riddle that is Rex Grossman and could not make up for putting too many youngsters on the field as a result of too many injuries.

The real culprit, though, was a skittish offense directed by Eli Manning that managed only 14 points, went scoreless after a 14-14 first half and actually gave up points when Manning's first interception of the season was returned for a touchdown for the Redskins, who are almost universally expected to finish last in the NFC East.

"I did not like the end of our game offensively at all," said Tom Coughlin, who called the operation "disorganized." As for losing on this, of all days, Coughlin said, "We knew the significance of the day and we wanted to pay our respects by the way in which we played."

The Giants had beaten the Redskins six straight and nine of last 10, but not this time. They put eight rookies on the field and the youngsters and the veterans all had a hand in the unsavory mix. It was 7-0 Giants after Manning's 68-yard pass to Hakeem Nicks led to Manning's roll-out touchdown run, and it was 14-7 Giants when a five-play, 85-yard drive ended on Ahmad Bradshaw's 6-yard run. Coverage lapses by cornerback Aaron Ross helped Grossman hit Anthony Armstrong in the end zone just 37 seconds before halftime to make it 14-14.

Two minutes into the second half, the Giants were behind for good. Facing third-and-15 on his own 15, Manning audibled

Giants defensive backs Kenny Phillips (left) and Tyler Sash take down Redskins tight end Fred Davis during the second half of the Giants' season-opening loss in Washington, D.C. (AP Images).

into a quick sideline pass to Nicks — and the Redskins snuffed it out. Right tackle Kareem McKenzie failed to cut-block linebacker Ryan Kerrigan, and the rookie from Purdue leaped over McKenzie and deflected Manning's pass up, snatched it out of the air for an interception and rumbled nine untouched yards for a touchdown.

"They typically don't [jump], they're normally trying to protect themselves," McKenzie said. "Kid made a great play, plain and simple. That's it."

Manning didn't see an alternative on the play.

"We were cutting that guy; he did a good move to avoid the cut, jump up and tip it up," Manning said. "Just a good play by him. Not a whole lot I can do about that."

Trailing 21-14 in the fourth quarter, the Giants seemed to get a lift when Jason Pierre-Paul's second sack of the game resulted in a Grossman fumble that Michael Boley scooped up and brought to the Washington 27-yard line. But the Giants couldn't muster a first down. Former Giants defensive tackle Barry Cofield chased down Ahmad Bradshaw on third down, and a 38-yard field goal attempt by Lawrence Tynes was blocked with 10:57 remaining.

"Defense put us in tremendous position to score, it's our job to score, especially from that distance," guard Chris Snee said.

"We just made the mistakes that Coach Coughlin continues to tell us that we can't make," Canty said. "We continue to do the things that he says we can't do. At some point, we as a team have got to listen." ■

Above: Hakeem Nicks carries the ball during the first half. Nicks led the Giants with seven catches for 122 yards, including a 68-yard reception that set up the game's first touchdown. Opposite: Giants defenders take down Redskins running back Tim Hightower during the first half. The Giants played well against the run, but allowed more than 300 passing yards. (AP Images)

REGULAR SEASON

SEPTEMBER 19, 2011 | GIANTS 28, RAMS 16

GIANTS BREATHE A SIGH OF RELIEF

Big Blue Earns Win Despite Maddeningly Inconsistent Night

By Paul Schwartz

The first order of business was successfully completed, with plenty of bumps and bruises along the way. No, the Giants are not doing much of anything with any hint of elegance or consistency, but they are no longer winless this season and that is a great relief to them.

There were stretches last night when Eli Manning could barely complete a pass or sniff a third-down conversion and even longer stretches when shoddy was too kind a description for the Giants' pass defense. Heck, Rams quarterback Sam Bradford piled up 321 passing yards — in the first three quarters.

There were some glimpses, though, that perhaps the Giants can get out of their own way often enough to accomplish something this season. They played unevenly and at times were unsightly, but they were fortunate the Rams were in the house as the Giants broke into the win column with a 28-16 victory in their home opener at MetLife Stadium.

Manning threw his first two touchdown passes of the season, but not before tossing an early interception that elicited plenty of boos.

The Giants were often torched by Bradford, but they did get a 65-yard touchdown return when linebacker Michael Boley scooped up a fumble and rambled down the sideline. The Giants did not have a defensive touchdown last season, so this is a sign of progress as they head into an NFC East clash on Sunday against the Eagles, who could be without Michael Vick, who has a concussion.

What was not a sign of progress was that Manning started out 2 for 11 for 19 yards (although he then completed 16 of his next 18). What also was reason for alarm is the way the Giants' secondary made the pedestrian Rams receivers look like the Greatest Show on Turf crew from years ago.

The Giants seemed to explode onto the scene as their offense raced 43 yards on five plays and looked as if they'd get a quick score when Mario Manningham ran free, seemingly beating safety Quintin Mikell. Manning, though, floated the ball, allowing Mikell all the time he needed to settle under it for an interception.

Next, the Giants looked amateurish on their first defensive series when Bradford hit a leaping Danario Alexander at the Giants' 30-yard line. Alexander had run past Aaron Ross and after he hit the turf he got back to his feet, with safety Deon

Grant standing right next to him. Grant never even tried to touch Alexander. Big mistake. Alexander scooted another 29 yards to the Giants' 1.

The defense stiffened, though, with Grant making amends by pressuring Bradford into an incompletion and the Rams had to settle for a 21-yard Josh Brown field goal for a 3-0 lead.

An ensuing three-and-out culminated with Manning getting booed rather loudly as he trotted off the field. He was saved by the Rams' ineptitude, though, as Greg Salas muffed a punt and Dave Tollefson recovered on the Rams' 38. A 23-yard pass interference penalty on cornerback Bradley Fletcher led to Manning's first scoring pass of the season, a 3-yarder to Hakeem Nicks, who made a nifty adjustment in the end zone to elude Fletcher.

Bradford got cooking again and the Rams got to the Giants' 7-yard line, but Ross tackled Salas short of a first down and another Brown field goal made it 7-6. It stayed that way through two Giants three-and-outs before Big Blue did something they hadn't done in nearly two full years.

Bradford, pressured into a quick throw by rookie linebacker Jacquian Williams, threw behind the line of scrimmage to Cadillac Williams, who dropped the ball and then stood around and looked at it. Boley did not. He did what he's been coached to do — scoop and score — and raced 65 yard for a touchdown to make it 14-6.

That was somewhat incredible, considering the Giants were being outgained 216-68. The Giants to that point also failed to convert their first six third-down attempts, making them 1-for-16 for the season.

Domenik Hixon made a case for himself late in the first half, batting the ball twice with his right hand in the end zone before securing it for the touchdown to make it 21-6 at halftime.

After Boley saved a Rams touchdown by deflecting a Bradford pass away and after another Rams field goal, Brandon Jacobs scored on a 9-yard run to increase the Giants' lead to 28-9.

Bradford hit Danario Alexander for a 19-yard touchdown over cornerback Michael Coe as the Rams pulled within 28-16 late in the third quarter. ∎

St. Louis defender Quintin Mikell intercepts a pass intended for Mario Manningham in the first quarter. This was the Giants only turnover as they collected their first win of the season. (N.Y. Post: Charles Wenzelberg)

REGULAR SEASON

SEPTEMBER 25, 2011 | GIANTS 29, EAGLES 16

DREAM ON!

Vick a Hurtin' Puppy as Giants Stun Eagles

By Paul Schwartz

Before he left for work, before the short trip to play a game yesterday few outside the Giants locker room believed there was much chance to win, Chris Snee received an unusual send-off.

"It's funny, the last thing my 5-year old said to me before I left to come to the stadium was 'Dad, you know these guys have beaten you six times in a row,'" Snee said. "I was like 'Thanks, Cooper, I know that.'"

The desultory losing skid to the despised Eagles came to a sudden and wholly unexpected halt because the Giants didn't care a bit for the credentials of their opponent, got a where-did-that-come-from performance from Victor Cruz (the first two touchdown receptions of his career), a brilliant rebound outing from cornerback Aaron Ross (two interceptions after he was benched last week), didn't rattle after a 14-0 lead became a 16-14 deficit and did exactly what they haven't been able to do — finish — in grand fashion, scoring the final 15 points to turn back the self-proclaimed Dream Team 29-16 and send the stunned fans at Lincoln Financial Field home in a sour mood.

"They can continue being the Dream Team and keep dreaming," Brandon Jacobs said. "That's all I can say."

Nothing can ever wipe away the stain of last year's epic collapse when a 31-10 fourth-quarter lead devolved into a shocking and historic 38-31 loss but, for now, the Giants are proud owners of a one-game winning streak over the Eagles after surviving a feisty and at times nasty game.

"We felt coming in that we could beat these guys because we should have last year," said Eli Manning, who finally put in a complete game, completing 16 of 23 passes for 254 yards and tied a career high with four touchdown passes, plus no interceptions.

Just like that, the Giants are 2-1, the Eagles are 1-2 and saw star quarterback-turned-mortal Michael Vick go down late in the third quarter with a broken right hand after completing a 23-yard pass to Jeremy Maclin and absorbing what he said was a late hit by Chris Canty.

"I was trying to protect myself, still didn't get a flag and that's pretty much been the story for the last three weeks," said Vick, who came back from suffering a concussion last week in Atlanta and played the first series of the fourth quarter with the broken hand before exiting for good.

A wild first half ended with the Giants somehow leading 14-13 after squandering nearly all of the 14-0 lead they built on Manning's 40-yard touchdown pass to Jacobs — who exploited rookie linebacker Casey Matthews in coverage — and a huge 74-yard catch-and-run by Cruz, making his first career start, replacing Mario Manningham (concussion).

The Giants didn't have many answers for running back LeSean McCoy (24 carries, 128 yeards, 1 TD) but they were toughest when it looked most grim, limiting the Eagles to a second-quarter field

Eli Manning reacts after Brandon Jacobs' successful two-point conversion run in the fourth quarter to give the Giants a 22-16 lead. (N.Y. Post: Charles Wenzelberg)

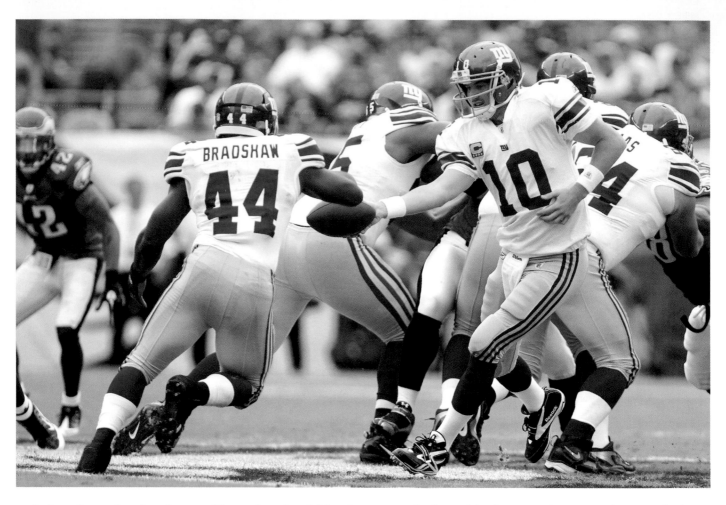

goal after a first-and-goal on the 3-yard line and another field goal after a first-and-goal at the Giants 2-yard line in the last minute of the third quarter.

Despite the second goal-line stand, the Eagles went up 16-14 — but not for long. Eagles coach Andy Reid, showing little regard for the Giants offense, eschewed a punt on fourth-and-1 from the Giants 43-yard line. Vick handed the ball to McCoy, who ran left, was slowed by safety Deon Grant and brought down by Michael Boley for a 3-yard loss with 11:38 remaining.

"They definitely thought that [the Giants offense couldn't take advantage] or else they wouldn't have done it," Grant said. "I'm glad they thought it."

It took Manning seven plays to make the Eagles pay, throwing one of those "oh no" passes into double coverage, trusting Cruz could make a play against safety Jarrad Page and all-world cornerback Nnamdi Asomugha. Cruz did, leaping over both defenders for a 28-yard scoring reception to make it 20-16.

Jacobs banged in the two-point conversion to make it 22-16. Reid went bold again, as Vick's replacement, Mike Kafka, on his first play fired deep downfield to DeSean Jackson but underthrew him and Ross came away with his second interception. With momentum squarely in their pocket, the Giants sealed the deal on a screen to Ahmad Bradshaw (15 carries, 86 yards), who scampered 18 yards to the end zone.

"If they're the Dream Team, what are we?" safety Antrel Rolle said.

"We definitely shut 'em up, there's no question about that," added Jacobs. "We walked off the field as the winners, and by a nice margin." ■

Above: Eli Manning hands off to Ahmad Brudshaw in the first quarter. Bradshaw led the Giants with 86 rushing yards and 53 receiving yards. Opposite: Eli Manning carries the ball in the third quarter. The Giants quarterback passed for four touchdowns in the win. (N.Y. Post: Charles Wenzelberg)

REGULAR SEASON

OCTOBER 2, 2011 | GIANTS 31, CARDINALS 27

GIANTS COME ALIVE IN DESERT STORM

Down 27-17, Eli Sparks Late Comeback

By Paul Schwartz

No one knew quite what to make of a game and a breakneck closing run that produced a stunning comeback victory replete with Eli Manning heroics, last-gasp defensive stops and an improbable play that could have gone either way but didn't.

That it came in the same venue where 1,336 days earlier the Giants somehow won Super Bowl XLII made a hard-to-believe game even more surreal as the Giants, trailing 27-17 with barely more than five minutes remaining, got two Manning touchdown passes in a span of 58 seconds and needed a late pass-breakup to beat the Cardinals 31-27 at University of Phoenix Stadium, now unofficially the most favorite place for the Giants to visit.

"I love this building," an ear-to-ear grinning co-owner John Mara told The Post in the same visitors' locker room where the Giants rejoiced after knocking off the Patriots following the 2007 season. "And I love this room."

That the game-winning touchdown catch, a 29-yarder from Manning to Hakeem Nicks with 2:39 remaining — came in the same left corner of the north end zone where Plaxico Burress scored for the decisive points in Super Bowl XLII turned a wild ride into a reminiscent one.

"It's a nice spot for us," general manager Jerry Reese decided.

This looked to be a wasted trip to the desert for the Giants (3-1), but instead it turned into another springboard after last week's emotional victory in Philadelphia.

The Giants, outplayed most of the afternoon, led 10-6 at halftime but trailed 20-10 after three quarters. They looked done when Beanie Wells, who ran through the Giants for a career-high 138 yards, scored his third rushing touchdown of the game with 5:16 remaining to put the Cardinals ahead 27-17.

"These guys never budged, they never folded and never hung their head, never doubted for one second," safety Antrel Rolle said.

Instead, Manning dipped into his bag of magic tricks and came up with not one, but two defining drives down the stretch as he completed 14 of 17 passes for 180 yards and two touchdowns in the fourth quarter. He hit tight end Jake Ballard to cut the deficit to 27-24 with 3:37 left and, with two time outs left, coach Tom Coughlin entrusted the game to his defense, which forced a three-and-out and used up only 27 seconds.

Manning, operating expertly out of the no-huddle offense, took over on the Cardinals' 48-yard line with 3:10 to go and no timeouts. Two plays and 31 seconds later, the Giants were in the end zone and regained the lead, but not without some angst and luck.

Tom Coughlin congratulates Brandon Jacobs after Jacobs' fourth-quarter touchdown. (AP Images)

A pass over the middle to Victor Cruz picked up 19 yards but in his haste to get down and save time, Cruz — untouched by a Cardinals defender — went to the ground and put the ball down. Cardinals cornerback Richard Marshall scooped it up for an apparent fumble recovery as the Cardinals rejoiced and Manning in disbelief put his hands to his helmet.

But referee Jerome Boger ruled that Cruz had given himself up, the play was over and the Cardinals could not challenge the ruling.

"We got a break on that one, I think," Manning said.

The Giants then made the break pay off. Manning had been harassed by the Cardinals' pressure but this time, as they came on a blitz, he had the protection he needed as he looked for and found Nicks deep down the left sideline, Nicks beating rookie cornerback Patrick Peterson for a 29-yard touchdown and the lead with 2:39 to go.

The Giants still had to play defense as the Cardinals took over with 2:35 remaining. They got a sack of Kevin Kolb by Osi Umenyiora — playing in his first game of the season — for a 10-yard loss and finished the grand comeback when cornerback Corey Webster on fourth down deflected Kolb's pass intended for Larry Fitzgerald.

"We just kept playing, we hung in there, we found a way to finish," Coughlin said. "We won the fourth quarter again, which we absolutely had to do.

"For us to come back and play like we did…it's a real testimony to the guys for just keeping on playing."

It was a wild finish and a dramatic victory for the Giants, who after losing their season-opener are 3-1 and tied with the Redskins for first place in the NFC East.

"We have a long way to go," Reese said, "but we're in good position right now." ■

Above: Giants tight end Jake Ballard hauls in a touchdown in the back of the end zone with 1:39 remaining in the fourth quarter. Opposite: Giants Center David Baas prepares to block the Cardinals' rush. (AP Images)

PICK-SIX TICKET COSTS BIG BLUE

Turnover Ends Giants Debacle

By Paul Schwartz

As bad as they looked all day, the Giants were going to find their way out of their own miserable ineptitude yesterday. They had finally taken a 25-22 lead with 4:49 remaining against the Seahawks, who history tell us are supposed to be asleep for early East Coast games like this.

Then the Giants found themselves behind 29-25, because their can't-stop-anything defense didn't stop Charlie Whitehurst from torching them with a you've-got-to-be kidding touchdown pass to a pathetically wide-open rookie Doug Baldwin.

Then the Giants seemingly were going to again rise up out of the mire of their dreary play. With 2:37 to go, Victor Cruz — Señor Excitement — was reaching down to haul in a 41-yard pass from Eli Manning and then a 19-yarder, and the Giants were on the Seattle 5-yard line with all the time in the world to punch in the winning points and get the heck out of MetLife Stadium with a hardly-earned victory.

Then they were doomed.

An inexcusable false start penalty on left tackle Will Beatty moved the ball back to the 10-yard line and the Giants finally got what they were angling for all afternoon. Manning looked left but his pass was too far ahead of Cruz, who initially slipped out of his break and tried to reach out with his left arm but only got his left hand on the ball, knocking it up into the air. Seattle

safety Kam Chancellor got a finger on the ball before cornerback Brandon Browner secured it and raced 94 yards for the clinching touchdown with 1:08 left to put the Giants out of their misery, and then into the misery of their 36-25 loss.

"About as miserable a feeling as we've had around here in a long time," surmised coach Tom Coughlin, who added, "When you don't deserve to win, you don't win."

No, they didn't deserve to win. Not even close. Riding high with a three-game winning streak, the Giants (3-2) were grasping and gasping from the very start. Manning passed for a career-high 420 yards and three touchdowns but also threw three interceptions — one on the chuck-it-up last possession with the game already gone. He — again — had no ground game (Ahmad Bradshaw, 58 yards) to fall back on.

The defense was worse. Tarvaris Jackson was getting things done well enough before he was knocked out of the game in the third quarter with a strained hip and Whitehurst (11 of 19, 149 yards) carved up a secondary that regressed. Once more, the run defense was suspect, with Marshawn Lynch needing only 12 carries to get 98 yards. A familiar problem came back to haunt the Giants, as they turned the ball over five times, with Manning and Cruz both losing fumbles. They also forgot how to block on a third-quarter disaster when defensive end Anthony Hargrove

stormed in to drop D.J. Ware in the end zone for a safety.

"As good as we have been playing the last couple of weeks, to come out here and lay an egg, 'embarrassing' is the only way I can think of it," defensive end Dave Tollefson said.

Despite themselves, the Giants were hanging in, probably because the Seahawks were letting them. A wild tip-to-himself reception for Cruz turned into a 68-yard catch-and-run for a touchdown and Bradshaw's two-point conversion run put the Giants ahead 22-19 early in the fourth quarter. They were up 25-22 with 4:49 remaining but the stop the Giants needed never came.

From the Giants 27-yard line, the Seahawks feasted on a monumental defensive blunder. Osi Umenyiora jumped offside

and for a moment it seemed as if the play was going to be whistled dead. It was only the coverage that was deceased. Aaron Ross and Antrel Rolle both moved to take Ben Obomanu running a curl to the inside, and neither bothered to even glance at Baldwin, who ran free as free can be as Whitehurst hit him for the game-winner.

"It was a miscommunication for the whole defense," Ross said. "Me and 'Trel jumped the same guy, jumped the outside guy. I guess it was bad communication."

Down 29-25, the Giants had plenty of time and all three timeouts and got to the Seattle 5-yard line before the Seahawks took it back to get what they deserved and give the Giants what they too deserved. ∎

Giants head coach Tom Coughlin and safety Derrick Martin react during the fourth quarter of the Giants' 36-25 loss to the Seahawks. (AP Images)

REGULAR SEASON

OCTOBER 16, 2011 | GIANTS 27, BILLS 24

CASHING IN BUFFALO CHIPS

Late Pick, FG Lift Giants to Pivotal Win

By Paul Schwartz

The game was there to be lost, and the Giants yesterday were on the verge of doing just that.

A back-and-forth battle was going the wrong way after a 24-17 fourth-quarter lead didn't grow because Mario Manningham couldn't hold on to a seeming touchdown catch, a field-goal attempt for a 10-point lead was blocked. And just like that the Bills were even at 24 after cornerback Corey Webster never turned around to contest Ryan Fitzpatrick's 9-yard scoring pass to Stevie Johnson.

"You want the chance, the opportunity to even the score," Webster said.

The lost lead was perilously close to becoming a lost game — and perhaps a lost season — when Eli Manning's offense went three-and-out, and back came the Bills, with Fitzpatrick hitting David Nelson for 32 yards. Just like that, they were on the Giants' 27-yard line, already in field-goal range, momentum seized, the crowd at sun-splashed MetLife Stadium poised for impending disaster.

"Never give up," cornerback Aaron Ross said. "They might make a play on us, but never get down. Just keep pushing and we know we're going to end up making a play if they keep throwing the ball on us."

The play the Giants desperately needed came when Webster leaped, turned his head and intercepted an underthrown Fitzpatrick pass on the left sideline intended for Johnson. Granted new life, Ahmad Bradshaw kick-started a late drive with a 30-yard run that resulted in a Lawrence Tynes 23-yard field goal. The Bills' last chance was snuffed out with Jason Pierre-Paul extending his long arms to deflect a Fitzpatrick pass and send it fluttering harmlessly to the ground, and the Giants had a 27-24 victory that was every bit as needed as it was difficult to attain.

"We made the plays when we had to make them," coach Tom Coughlin said.

"This is a big-play league," said linebacker Michael Boley. "One play can either make or break a game at any moment."

And one game can dramatically alter the course of a season.

The Giants, a week after a desultory loss to the Seahawks, are 4-2 entering their bye week, alone in first place in the NFC East, expecting to get Justin Tuck and several other key players back from injury in time to face the Dolphins the day before Halloween before a murderers' row stretch of games.

"Guys made plays and a big win ... 4-2, feels like we're in a good spot," Manning said.

Ahmad Bradshaw celebrates after his third-quarter touchdown that gave the Giants a 24-17 lead. (N.Y. Post: Charles Wenzelberg)

Getting this one was about as tough as it gets, as the Bills (4-2), after trailing 7-0, struck back quickly and decisively. First it was an 80-yard touchdown run by Fred Jackson and then a 60-yard scoring pass to Naaman Roosevelt on a blown coverage for 140 yards and 14 points worth of damage on only two plays.

The key for the Giants was Manning's ability to protect the ball against the NFL's best defense in causing turnovers (16 in the first five games). Manning was an effective 21 of 32 for 292 yards and finally got some support on the ground, with Bradshaw (26 carries, a season-high 104 yards) scoring a career-high three touchdowns, all on 1-yard runs. The Giants did not turn the ball over once.

"I'm proud of the guys," Manning said. "We played smart football."

Bradshaw took off and leaped into the end zone to make it a 24-17 third-quarter lead for the Giants, but Webster's first interception of Fitzpatrick — who under-threw Johnson on the left sideline — wasn't turned into points by the Giants. That set up the tense closing minutes and, for the Giants, a winning closing act. Jackson gained 121 yards but only 14 in the second half.

"Finish what we started," Coughlin said. "We talked a lot about positive energy this week because obviously there was a lot of negative out there and I think the players responded to that."

Osi Umenyiora, with one of three sacks against Fitzpatrick, chuckled when asked if Webster's second interception was a season-saving moment.

"No, it's too early to be talking about season-savers," Umenyiora said. "It was just a great play by him. You never know which play is going to make or break your season. It's huge. We had to go into our bye week with a win." ∎

Above: Hakeem Nicks hauls in an Eli Manning pass during the first half. Nicks led the Giants with four catches for 96 yards. Opposite: Ahmad Bradshaw goes airborne over Buffalo defender Jairus Byrd. (N.Y. Post: Charles Wenzelberg)

HIS OWN MANN

Finally Out of Peyton's Shadow, Clutch Eli Is Illuminating His Own Place in Playoff History

By Mike Vaccaro

Ben is a Roethlisberger. Drew is a Brees. Aaron is a Rodgers. None of them was burdened by a birth certificate, defined by their DNA. Joe was a Namath. Johnny was a Unitas. Otto was a Graham. They were judged by what they did, not what their brothers did, not by who their fathers were.

Tom is a Brady.

Joe is a Flacco.

Alex is a Smith.

If any of them leads his team to victory this weekend, leads his team to Indianapolis for a date in the Super Bowl, he gets to make the trip without context, without qualification. For Brady it would be another line on top of a crowded Hall of Fame résumé, for Smith the ultimate redemption for those who pegged him an epic failure, for Flacco another step in separating himself from the crowded middle tier of B-list quarterbacks.

But Eli is a Manning and he's been a Manning from birth, and if there probably were moments as a kid when that helped — no Pop Warner coach in New Orleans is going to make a kid named Manning play left tackle, after all — most of his adult life it has meant dealing with being the scion of the Quarterback Kennedys.

At Ole Miss, opposing fans dElighted in chanting "Peyton's better!" at him. For the first half of his professional career, every time he threw a ball to the wrong jersey or led a failed fourth-quarter comeback or lost a home playoff game he had to endure chapter and verse about how this is why Peyton is the better quarterback or that is why Eli never will measure up.

Most quarterbacks get to fail on their own. Eli's failures always came accompanied by a little more: more venom, more vigor, more told-you-so.

"Eli's always been tough," said Cooper Manning, the brother who decided to break with the family business and play receiver at Ole Miss, the other day inside a crowded and dElirious Giants locker room at Lambeau Field, after watching Eli lead the Giants past the Packers. "You don't do what he's chosen to do, play that position, and not have a little brass in your blood."

Cooper, the oldest of Archie and Olivia's three boys, the one whose football aspirations ended when he was diagnosed with a narrowing of the spinal canal, smiled.

"And this," he said, "is as confident as I've ever seen him play. This is an offense that's geared toward a quarterback taking control. And Eli is stepping up to the plate."

We automatically compare Eli with Peyton, because of the bloodlines. But he has now beaten Brady and Rodgers heads-up with seasons on the line. He beat Brett Favre, too. Not so long

Eli Manning throws as pass during the Giants' September 19 win over the Rams. Eli Manning won his second Super Bowl, one more than his brother, Peyton. (N.Y. Post: Charles Wenzelberg)

ago, there were some who liked to argue Tony Romo was the better quarterback; Eli chased Romo out of the 2008 playoffs and ended the Cowboys' season this year.

For years, Peyton's great white whale was Brady; Eli has no nemesis to speak of. For every game Peyton has played, he has had at least one target who either will be a surefire or borderline Hall of Famer (Marvin Harrison and Reggie Wayne and Dallas Clark); the remarkable thing about Eli is that his rotating corps of receivers always seems to elevate to his will. Maybe Victor Cruz and Hakeem Nicks would be good on their own, but with Eli they have become game-breakers. That much we do know.

See, here's the problem with wandering too close to this fire:

In the same way it has minimized Eli all these years to be compared with Peyton, it works the same way in reverse. Peyton's legacy — his legend — should not be diminished just because his younger, healthier brother has become his own man.

"I don't think it insults either one to say they're both outstanding," Packers coach Mike McCarthy said last week, before discovering just how correct he was.

It doesn't. Eli is a Manning. Peyton is a Manning. If one were a Flacco and the other a Smith, they still would be what they are: as good at the position as the position allows.

And the Giants wouldn't swap their Manning. Not for a Brees. Not for a Brady. Or for anyone else named Manning, either. ■

Above: Eli Manning eyes a receiver during the Giants' October 30 win over the Dolphins. Opposite: Manning assesses the situation during New York's come-from-behind win over Buffalo in October. (N.Y. Post: Charles Wenzelberg)

REGULAR SEASON

OCTOBER 30, 2011 | GIANTS 20, DOLPHINS 17

GIANTS BENEFIT FROM MIAMI'S VICE

Winless Fish Throw Big Scare into Big Blue

By Paul Schwartz

Osi Umenyiora was hanging around the X-ray room after the Giants had just barely disposed of the winless Dolphins when he saw that the Rams had broken out of the winless column by upsetting the Saints.

"So you never know what's going to happen," Umenyiora said. "There's no such thing about playing down or playing up. You win by one or you win by 20, you win."

For the better part of three hours yesterday, the winning part was somehow escaping the Giants, who were hearing it from the crowd of 79,302 for repeated blunders and for keeping the Dolphins not only in the game but ahead. A 7-0 deficit became a 14-3 deficit and the Giants still trailed 17-10 heading into the fourth quarter. It was the day before Halloween and the home team was scaring the heck out of its paying customers.

"You go out and start a little flat and let them get some energy and this is what happens, you're in a game," guard Chris Snee said.

Even though Umenyiora said: "I never honestly had any doubt we were going to win, I knew we'd come alive at some point," it sure didn't feel that way inside MetLife Stadium. The Giants needed an Eli Manning touchdown pass to fan favorite Victor Cruz with 5:58 remaining and then they finally put the clamps down with some fearsome defensive pressure to secure a 20-17 victory over a Dolphins club that is now 0-7.

"When there are opportunities to win games you have to take them," Manning said. "I think we are doing good jobs of finding ways to win."

That the Giants (5-2) had to find a way to win against a team that firmly is a top contender for the Andrew Luck sweepstakes is disturbing, especially considering what comes next. The Giants face the Patriots on Sunday, the start of a brutal five-game stretch, and there is no conceivable way the performance they put in to barely subdue the Dolphins is going to cut it with the steep rise in competition.

"We weren't as sharp as we thought we were going to be," Tom Coughlin said.

The Giants showed no outward signs of relief and the only reason they won may be that they had Manning and the Dolphins did not. Manning again was brilliant on a day when the Giants had no running game (50 yards from Ahmad Bradshaw, 10 from rusty Brandon Jacobs). Manning was forced into a season-high 45 passes and he completed 31 of them for 349 yards with touchdowns to Mario Manningham and Cruz. Once again, Manning did not throw an interception and at times he was the only reason why the Giants were even in the game.

"He lit it up," Cruz said.

Eli Manning throws as pass in the fourth quarter. The Giants quarterback completed 31 passes for 349 yards in the win.
(N.Y. Post: Charles Wenzelberg)

"It was clearly one of those days running the ball was just not happening for us, so you got to go with what's working," added Snee. "Eli was extremely hot and our receivers were getting open."

Trailing 14-3, Manning directed an 84-yard drive that ended with his 7-yard scoring pass to Manningham just eight seconds before halftime to cut the margin to 14-10, but Dan Carpenter's 40-yard field goal made it 17-10 early in the third quarter. From there, the Giants finally clamped down on Bush (15-103), stopped getting burned by Moore's scrambling and made the Dolphins look like the inept offense they have shown themselves to be.

A 29-yard field goal by Lawrence Tynes pulled the Giants within 17-13 early in the fourth quarter and the winning points came when Manning from the Miami 25-yard line found Cruz (7-99) over the middle. Cruz eluded cornerback (and former Giant) Will Allen at the 10-yard line, spun out of an Allen tackle attempt at the 5-yard line and lunged into the end zone.

Sacks by Mathias Kiwanuka, Justin Tuck and Umenyiora in the last two Dolphins possessions led to Corey Webster's game-clinching interception.

"You have to be able to go out there and play as an underdog, but you also have to be able to go out there and play when you're favored," Kiwanuka said. "That's something we're still learning. I think we took a big step today, but we've got to get to that point where we can go out there and smash everybody in the face no matter what." ▪

Above: Hakeem Nix stays in bounds on a 13-yard third-quarter reception. Opposite: Giants tackle Linval Joseph sacks Dolphins quarterback Matt Moore in the fourth quarter. (N.Y. Post: Charles Wenzelberg)

REGULAR SEASON

NOVEMBER 6, 2011 | GIANTS 24, PATRIOTS 20

HURTS SO GOOD

Injury-Riddled Giants Stun Pats in Thriller

By Paul Schwartz

Before the sounds of victory, there was the sight of victory — Brandon Jacobs unable to hold back. Inside the visitors' locker room in the Gillette Stadium home that is usually invulnerable for the Patriots, Jacobs lifted his head coach into the air as Tom Coughlin was about to laud the Giants for the effort they just put forth.

This doesn't happen often in early November, but after what guard David Diehl described as "one of the biggest regular-season wins I've ever been involved in," there was no holding back.

"Coughlin's a little heavy," Jacobs said.

"We got carried away," admitted Justin Tuck. "It brings back memories. We were happy about that."

A beaming Coughlin said, "I was thinking they were going to drop me on my head."

There was no dropping of anything yesterday after the Giants reached the midpoint of their season with as thrilling and chilling a game as they've played since, well, Super Bowl XLII when they shocked the world by knocking off the undefeated Patriots. This time, it was the unbeatable (at home) Patriots — winners of 20 straight regular-season home games — that were done in by not one but two last-minute epic Eli Manning drives, with a crushing defensive failure sandwiched in between to add another layer of drama to what ultimately unfolded into a wild 24-20 triumph.

"We did something that hasn't been done in a long time, they

haven't lost here since 2008," safety Antrel Rolle said. "We came in and beat them at their field."

Manning's 1-yard touchdown pass to tight end Jake Ballard with 15 seconds remaining gave the Giants (6-2) their winning points, after Tom Brady found his own tight end, Rob Gronkowski, with just 1:36 left to give the Patriots a 20-17 lead. That was after Manning, with 3:03 to go, hit Mario Manningham on a 10-yard scoring pass to put the Giants ahead 17-13. It was a rousing closing finish after these two teams slugged it out through a scoreless first half — the first 0-0 halftime score in the NFL this season — and then erupted for 44 second-half points, with 31 coming in the fourth quarter and 21 coming in the last 3:03.

Manning admitted he couldn't avoid a flashback to his game-winning drive four years ago in Super Bowl XLII, when he again needed a two-minute drill to fend off a late Brady touchdown pass.

"I'd rather be down by three with 1:30 left than up four with 1:30 to go and Tom Brady on the field," Manning said. "I think you like those situations where you have the opportunity to win the game."

Few are doing that any better this season than Manning. The Giants led 10-0 in the third quarter and could have extended a 10-3 lead when Manning, already in field goal range deep in New England territory, made his one glaring mistake, lofting a pass to Manningham that was intercepted in the end zone by

Jason Pierre-Paul pressures Tom Brady in the second quarter. The Giants defense sacked Brady twice and recorded two interceptions. (N.Y. Post: Charles Wenzelberg)

cornerback Kyle Arrington. On the sideline, Coughlin could be seen wincing and saying "Don't do that!"

After intercepting Brady twice and keeping him at bay, the Giants defense couldn't hold him off forever. Brady hit Aaron Hernandez on a 5-yard touchown and Steven Gostkowski hit a 45-yard field goal for a 13-10 Patriots lead midway through the fourth quarter. Showing his mettle, Manning took offense — playing without his top receiver (Hakeem Nicks), runner (Ahmad Bradshaw) and starting center (David Baas)—85 yards, hitting Manningham to make it 17-13.

That potential game-winning comeback drive didn't stick. Brady in nine plays went 64 yards and on fourth-and-9 from the Giants 14-yard line found Gronkowski, who eluded linebacker Michael Boley for what looked to be the clincher with only 1:36 left.

"You're kind of sick to your stomach at that point," Tuck said. "It's kind of like, if you've ever been like real amped about

something and all of a sudden something happens and you just come crashing down. I had a throbbing headache at that point. As [bad] as you're feeling you still understand we're putting the ball [in the hands of] one of the best quarterbacks in the league."

Manning guided the Giants 80 yards, hitting Ballard on a 28-yard pass to get things moving. A key 35-yard pass interference penalty on safety Sergio Brown mauling Victor Cruz with 30 seconds left put the Giants on the New England 1-yard line. From there, it took Manning three plays to hit paydirt, when on third down he found Ballard, who beat linebacker Tracy White in the left corner of the end zone for the game-winning catch with just 15 seconds left.

Kind of like what Manning did to win Super Bowl XLII.

"It played out like that, didn't it?" Tuck said. "Eli's just a fantastic quarterback, he's playing outstanding and he carried it home for us today." ▪

Above: Brandon Jacobs runs into the end zone on a 10-yard touchdown run in the third quarter to give the Giants a 10-0 lead. Opposite: Tight end Jake Ballard completes a 30-yard reception in the third quarter. The play set up the first score of the game, a Lawrence Tynes field goal. (N.Y. Post: Charles Wenzelberg)

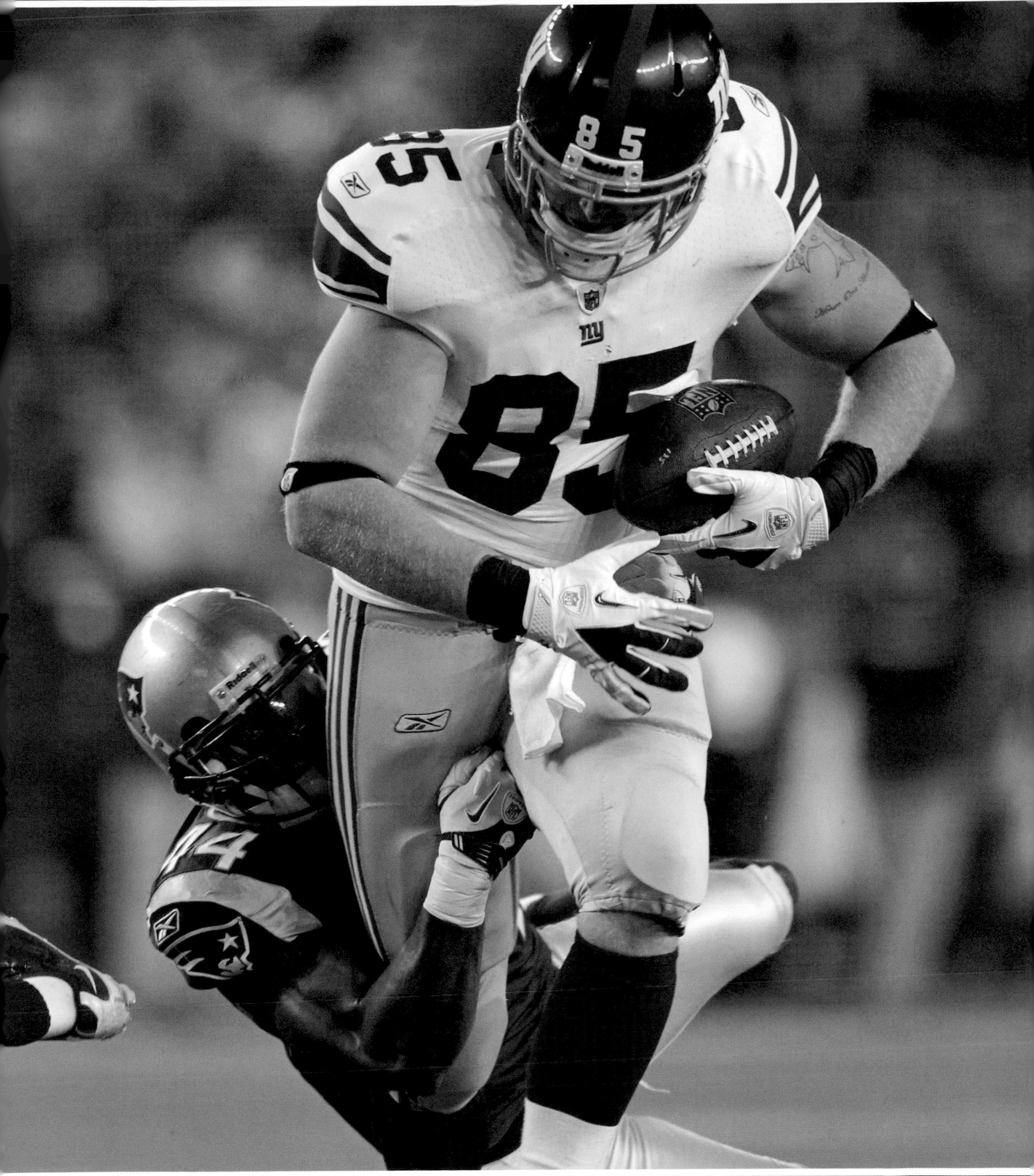
85
ny
85

MANNING SIMPLY SUPER WHEN IT MATTERS

BY STEVE SERBY

Nearly four years later, nearly four years after the shining moment of his football life, nearly four years after he engineered the game-winning drive that beat Tom Brady and ruined Bill Belichick's perfect season, here stood Eli Manning inside a raucous Gillette Stadium.

The scoreboard read Patriots 20, Giants 17.

The clock read 1:36.

Not Glendale, Ariz., in February.

Foxborough, Mass., in November.

But Eli Manning, on Daylight Savings Time, turned back the clock anyway.

Eli Manning, eyeball to eyeball with Brady, didn't blink this time either.

The elite quarterback of the Giants beat the elite quarterback of the Patriots once again, 24-20 this time.

There was no hoisting of the Lombardi Trophy this time.

Just a hoisting of Tom Coughlin in a jubilant visiting room by proud, underdog, defiant, Giants who felt nothing short of Super.

Brady, starting from his 36 with 2:58 left, had just rifled a fourth-and-9, 14-yard touchdown pass to Rob Gronkowski against Michael Boley.

As the PAT teams lined up, Dave Tollefson had a warning for Patriots offensive linemen.

"You left too much time on the clock," Tollefson said.

He later said: "That's how confident I am in Eli."

Manning started at his 20.

No Ahmad Bradshaw.

No Hakeem Nicks.

No David Tyree.

No Plaxico Burress.

No problem.

"We gotta score.... We got time.... Just be calm.... We're gon-na get it done," Manning said.

Manning trailed 14-10 when he took the ball at the 17 in the Super Bowl with 2:39 and three timeouts left.

"Obviously it's a little different when we're down three in that situation, not four.... We could have settled for a field goal," Manning said.

He wanted the touchdown. Manning found Victor Cruz for 19 yards.

"He doesn't get flustered at all," Cruz said, "he showed amazing confidence and amazing resolve. And...I'm just glad he's on my side."

Manning, on third-and-10, found tight end Jake Ballard, who used his 6-foot-6 body to reach up for the ball and hold on after contact for a 28-yard gain.

Ballard wears No. 85.

Tyree wore No. 85.

"You know what to expect.... You know what all the terms are.... Those are fun situations to be in," Manning said. "As an athlete, as a quarterback, you want the ball in your hands at the end of the game. I'd rather be down by three with 1:30 than up by four with 1:30 with Tom Brady, with their offense on the field. You like those situations where you have an opportunity to go win the game."

Manning scrambled for 12 more. The Giants called their second timeout. Thirty-five seconds on the clock. Manning looked deep for Cruz and got interference on Sergio Brown.

First-and-goal at the 1.

Now third-and-goal at the 1.

NYG timeout No. 3.

Ninteeen seconds left.

Manning-to-Ballard, against Tracy White.

Fifteen seconds on the clock.

Giants 24, Patriots 20.

Not Glendale, Ariz., in February.

Foxborough, Mass., in November.

But it sure felt like Super Bowl XLII.

Deja Blue.

The Giants had pounded Brady, rattled him, intercepted him twice, forced a fumble. But then a fumbled punt by Aaron Ross and an end-zone interception of Manning by Kyle Arrington gave the Pats life.

Now it was the fourth quarter.

Brady versus Manning four years later.

Manning, down 13-10, started at his 15. The clock read 7:04.

Manning got 35 yards when Arrington interfered with Mario Manningham. Third-and-5 from the 10, he looked left for Manningham, against Arrington, in the back of the end zone.

Giants 17, Patriots 13.

Same corner where Burress caught the game-winner in Super Bowl XLII.

3:03 left this time.

"It just seems like no matter what he does, somebody's gonna always say something bad about him or not believe in him or whatever it may be, just because everybody considers his brother to be the elite quarterback," Justin Tuck said. "Look at what he's done in this league.... I think what makes him so calm in that situation is the fact that he knows, regardless of what everybody else is saying, he knows that these guys in his locker room believe in him. I think deep down in his heart, he doesn't want to let us down."

Brady's turn.

"Kinda a role reversal there.... Fortunately enough, they scored it real quick," Manning said.

Patriots fans holding signs that Manning was no elite quarterback would soon leave shell-shocked.

"I don't make a habit of looking into the stands or reading their signs," Manning said, "and if I did, I don't think I would have thought they were the expert to make that decision."

Brandon Jacobs, who lifted a joyous Coughlin, said: "If there are any fans in the NFL who should know Eli is elite, it should be these fans."

SuperMann in Glendale, Ariz., SuperMann in Foxborough, Mass. ∎

Above: Eli Manning hands the ball off to Brandon Jacobs in the first quarter. Manning completed 20 of 39 passes for 250 yards and two touchdowns as the Giants upset the favored Patriots in Foxborough, Massachusetts. (N.Y. Post: Charles Wenzelberg)

REGULAR SEASON

NOVEMBER 13, 2011 | 49ERS 27, GIANTS 20

4TH & WRONG

Giants Last Gasp Falls Short After Niners Score 15 Points in 61 Secs

By Paul Schwartz

The march was on, Eli Manning firing left and right, converting fourth-down passes to Mario Manningham and Victor Cruz, making like the fourth-quarter marksman he has been all season. The Giants were trailing the rugged 49ers, but the Giants figured they had them right where they wanted them.

"I thought we were in perfect control and I thought we would get there, score, send it into overtime and win it in overtime," coach Tom Coughlin said, far more matter-of-factly than the situation seemed to warrant.

Coughlin has seen it all season, witnessed Manning's late-game heroics and here they were again, the Giants advancing to the 49ers 10-yard line, having narrowly missed the tying points when a deep ball just barely glanced off the outstretched hands of Manningham for what would have been a game-tying 42-yard scoring pass.

You play with fire often enough, though, eventually you get burned. Manning and the Giants could not finish what they started, ultimately couldn't overcome two Niners touchdowns in a 61-second span and when a last-gasp pass was batted away by defensive tackle Justin Smith with 34 seconds left the Giants knew they had to exit Candlestick Park on the wrong end of a 27–20 loss that many Giants believe is not the last time they will see this particular opponent again.

"They pulled it out this time," receiver Hakeem Nicks said.

"It was a dogfight and I can't say nothing bad about 'em," added Brandon Jacobs. "I do know we're going to see them again. We're going to see the San Francisco 49ers again."

That is for another day. In the here and now, the Giants (6-3) saw their hold on first place in the NFC East trimmed to a one-game lead on the Cowboys (5-4) and this Sunday have a chance to put the reeling Eagles (3-6) out of their misery for good. On their long flight home, the Giants no doubt considered the many ways they could have returned from the West Coast winners rather than frustrated losers.

Manning completed his first 10 passes, but the Giants trailed a field goal-fest 9-6 at halftime and 12-6 early in the third quarter before they finally found the end zone on Manning's 13-yard pass to Manningham, who made an over-the-shoulder grab behind rookie cornerback Chris Culliver and dragged his feet before running out of bounds. The Giants, specialists in winning when trailing after three quarters, were up 13-12 entering the final quarter.

It all came awry fairly quickly. Steve Weatherford, so consistent this season, miss-hit a punt that sailed just 29 yards

San Francisco receiver Vernon Davis catches a 31-yard touchdown in the fourth quarter as the 49ers took the lead in their 27-20 victory over the Giants. (AP Images)

out of bounds to put the Niners at the 50.

"Way out of bounds and way too short," bemoaned Coughlin.

Soon enough, Alex Smith was hitting tight end Vernon Davis for a 31-yard catch-and-run touchdown, as rookie linebacker Greg Jones blew the assignment and stayed inside as Davis ran a crossing route. Smith hit Michael Crabtree on the 2-point conversion to put the 49ers up 20-13.

"I got to take full responsibility for that, that's my man," Jones said.

Two plays later, Manning and Manningham weren't on the same page, the receiver thinking the quarterback was scrambling, causing Manningham to cut off his route as the pass was thrown over the middle, where there was no Giants player and cornerback Carlos Rogers made a diving interception on the Giants 17-yard line. Earlier, a Rogers interception off Manning did not cost the Giants but this time it did. On the next play, rookie Kendall Hunter scooted 17 yards for a touchdown

to make it 27-13 with 12:21 left.

"We always feel we are always in the game," said Manning.

Manning completed an 80-yard drive with a 32-yard touchdown pass to Hakeem Nicks to cut the deficit to 27-20 with 8:37 remaining. The Giants got the ball back and Eli went to work again. He completed fourth down passes to Manningham and Victor Cruz and in between nearly got a 42-yard touchdown when a deep ball down the middle glanced just off Mannigham's outstretched hands at the 3-yard line.

The final drive made it to the 49ers 10-yard line but no further. The Giants needed just two yards for a first down but came up empty. Manning swore he saw Cruz open and tight end Jake Ballard couldn't escape the clutches of linebacker Patrick Willis, leaving Ballard and Cruz in the same area. No matter. The last pass was batted down at the line by Justin Smith with just 34 seconds left. ∎

Above: Jake Ballard dives for extra yardage in the second quarter. Opposite: The Giants defense faces off against the 49ers offense in the first quarter. The 49ers were limited to just three field goals in the first half. (AP Images)

OFF AND RUNNING

Giants' New Daddy Cruz Star of the Home Team

By Brad Hamilton

Becoming a father last week meant more to Giants wide receiver Victor Cruz than to many first-time dads. The birth of his daughter, Kennedy, occurred just as Cruz has emerged as an NFL superstar, something his father predicted years ago.

But dad Mike Walker, a hero firefighter in Paterson, NJ, died under mysterious circumstances in 2007 — and has missed it all.

"It's definitely bittersweet," said Cruz, who delivers a silent prayer to Walker in the end zone before each kickoff. "It's been such a great year so far. I know he's looking down and he's proud."

How could anyone argue with that?

Cruz, an undrafted free agent from a humble college program who hadn't caught a regular-season pass before this year, set a club record with 1,536 receiving yards, including a dazzling, 99-yard TD, the longest scoring play in Giants history.

That sudden success, plus his signature salsa-dance touchdown celebrations and his constant, beaming smile, has charmed Giants fans and spurred hopes for more hip swiveling today when the team takes on the Green Bay Packers in Wisconsin.

It all has Cruz thinking about how far he's come — and the importance of being a good father.

When longtime girlfriend Elaina Watley gave birth Monday, "I cried a little and had a feeling I've never had before," he said.

And then he broke into a salsa, using the moves his maternal grandmother taught him as a kid.

"It was a few minutes after when I started dancing."

If you drive 15 minutes north from MetLife Stadium, you come to East 18th Street and 11th Avenue in Paterson, a block infested with drugs and gangs. On one corner is Joe's, a cut-rate liquor store and check-cashing service. Across the street is a white, one-story house with peeling paint and a chain-link fence.

That's where Cruz, 25, grew up, with his beloved mother, Blanca Cruz, and half-sister, Andrea, now a 17-year-old high-school student.

"It was rough," Cruz has said. "You would hear gunshots at night while you were sleeping. You would hear police chases."

Drugs were a steady lure.

"It's easy to get sucked into that life," he said. "I was [tempted]. But I had a good support system, and my mom always knew there was bigger and better things out there for me."

Walker, however, didn't live with the Cruz family. He was across town with his wife, Jacqueline, and two other children, Ebony, a daughter, and Malik, a son.

But Walker devoted himself to both sets of kids.

Victor Cruz points after catching a pass in the Giants' upset win over the Green Bay Packers in the NFC Divisional Playoffs. Cruz caught five passes for 74 yards as the Giants upset the NFL's best regular-season team. (N.Y. Post: Charles Wenzelberg)

"He would come visit all the time and take me and my brother out," said Cruz. "He was an intricate part of my life."

Sports helped. Cruz's first love was karate — he once leaped over 10 people to break a board. And by the time he was a 5-foot-9 teen, he could dunk.

But he found his true calling with the Paterson FD Bulldogs, a team of 12-year-olds coached by his dad — after a rough start.

"He had us using double pads so thick we could hardly move," recalled Malik. "It was the typical overprotective parent but who also happens to be the coach."

After a stellar career at Paterson Catholic HS, where his team went 11-0 in 2003 and won a state championship, Cruz got a full scholarship to the University of Massachusetts, where he finished with 131 career catches.

But while Cruz was away at college, his father's life was falling to pieces — in part because of mistreatment by the Paterson Fire Department, where he'd spent 23 years and was honored several times, his colleagues and friends said.

On one occasion, Walker saved the life of a 3-year-old baby after the child stopped breathing, said firefighter Andrew Selby. On another, he led Selby to safety while fighting a house fire so thick with heat and smoke that "you would have died if you stood up."

"He was a motivator. People wanted him in their company. And he was ripped — he had the body of a 22-year-old," Selby said.

But while driving on Route 20 in the winter of 2006, Walker flipped his Mercedes convertible and broke his back and neck. His supervisors forced him back on the job shortly after, putting him in charge of delivering supplies to firehouses, a job that required heavy lifting. He was eventually fired, amid charges of racial discrimination. He then got sick.

"Mike was broke and he was physically deteriorating," said Selby.

Walker was found dead in his apartment in Passaic on March 1, 2007. His death was reported by the press as a suicide, but Selby doubts that.

"When I came into the apartment, the police were just there. Mike was on the floor near the bedroom. It looked like he was clutching for the door. I don't know where the suicide conclusion came from."

Cruz got the news from Malik, who called him and broke down in tears.

"I hung up the phone and took a moment," Cruz said. "Just sat back and didn't understand it."

Cruz's emergence on the field is complemented by a perpetual grin and friendly openness, and a humility not often seen in an NFL star.

A Paterson neighbor named Dennis, a retiree, recalled approaching Blanca Cruz last summer. He was going door to door looking for work. She hired him to clean up the yard.

Her son, he told a reporter, came by and asked if he needed help trimming the hedges.

"He gave me some tools. Very nice kid," he said.

He didn't know the nice kid was a Giants wide receiver — until the reporter informed him.

"You mean it's *the* Victor Cruz?" he asked.

There was much joy this week at Cruz's apartment in Lyndhurst, where Cruz's mom and his girlfriend Elaina — a voluptuous but down-to-earth beauty who grew up in Englewood, NJ — soaked up time with the baby.

Kennedy herself seemed OK with all the attention — she slept through her first night and allowed her proud pop a full eight hours.

"She didn't cry too much," Cruz said. "I was able to bring her home and put her into my bed and speak to her a little bit."

Cruz has been getting plenty of advice, including a call from his old high-school football coach, Benjie Wimberly.

"I told him, 'When you become a dad, that's reality,'" Wimberly said.

"This is bigger than winning the Super Bowl."

Then again, why not have it all? ■

Victor Cruz celebrates after Hakeem Nicks catches a touchdown pass in the Giants' playoff win over the Packers at Lambeau Field. (N.Y. Post: Charles Wenzelberg)

REGULAR SEASON

NOVEMBER 20, 2011 | EAGLES 17, GIANTS 10

BIRD BRAINS

Bumbling Big Blue Falls to Eagles
By Paul Schwartz

Goodbye, first place. Hello, second-half swoon.

It's another season and the Giants are in form, descending in the standings, allowing the Eagles to come into their house and administer a crushing blow. These Birds who arrived at MetLife Stadium last night were a wounded bunch, but they had enough to flyover the Giants 17-10 in a game that should prompt all the requisite panic about this Giants season threatening to slip away.

Manhandled on offense and picked apart late on defense, the Giants were clearly the less-inspired team, and that did not sit well at all with coach Tom Coughlin.

"As big a disappointment as we've had around here in a long time," he said.

There was no Michael Vick and no Jeremy Maclin, and the Eagles came in reeling at 3-6 and in last place. But they still were too much for the slip-sliding Giants, whose offense was dreadful almost all evening, ranging from anemic to unproductive to unwatchable. They managed only 29 rushing yards.

"Which is as pathetic as it can get," Coughlin said.

"OK, we can use his word pathetic," guard Chris Snee said.

After Manning finally got the Giants in the end zone to tie the game at 10 in fourth quarter with a 24-yard touchdown pass to Victor Cruz, the Giants defense caved in, unable to contain backup quarterback Vince Young, who converted an incredible six third downs.

Young cashed in when he drilled an 8-yard touchdown pass to Riley Cooper, who beat Deon Grant, with 2:54 left for the winning points. The Eagles took 18 plays and burned 8:51 on the clock to go 80 yards.

"Our defense did some good things in the first half, but our defense in the second half was really not very good," Coughlin said.

The final, fleeting chance for the Giants was extinguished when defensive end Jason Babin was pushed up in the pocket by right tackle Kareem McKenzie, directly into Manning, who was sacked and fumbled the ball away with 1:17 left. It was recovered by defensive tackle Derek Landri, and that was that. Before that, Manning's 47-yard pass to Cruz put the Giants on the Eagles' 21-yard line.

The loss completely obliterates what was once a solid lead in the NFC East. The Giants, losers of two straight, and the hot Cowboys, winners of three straight, are tied atop the division at 6-4, but the Giants are actually in second place, as the Cowboys have a better division record (1-1 for the Giants, 2-1 for Dallas).

The Giants don't like to hear about their meltdowns under Coughlin, but they are now 0-2 in the second half and they face a brutal schedule ahead, with a game in New Orleans followed by a meeting with the unbeaten Packers.

Afterward, Coughlin said he instructed the players to look in the mirror. "My question for them is, 'Why?'" Coughlin said.

Giants cornerback Aaron Ross intercepts a Vince Young pass in the end zone. Young threw three interceptions, but the Eagles prevailed 17-10. (N.Y. Post: Charles Wenzelberg)

"What does it take to understand what the Eagles were going to be like coming here? You don't have to be a rocket scientist to know that the team is 3-6 with their backs to the wall, they are going to play their butts off."

What sickened Coughlin was how his club at times was meek against the desperate Eagles. After rookie Prince Amukamara in his NFL debut got a first-quarter interception, Manning had Cruz open but couldn't get the ball over linebacker Jamar Chaney for a gift interception.

On Chaney's return, defensive tackle Trevor Laws leveled Manning — who was not in the play — with a cheap shot, prompting Snee to go wild in the first of two altercations he instigated. There were offsetting penalties called on the play.

"Instead of the team rallying around when the quarterback got hit when the guy drove the quarterback in the back, you would think your team would rally but we didn't do that," Coughlin said. "We had someone come forward and try to retaliate."

Snee, who played with a stomach bug that made him sick between plays before he was finally forced out with dehydration, said, "I saw Trevor take a shot at [Manning] and I didn't like it. Our job is to protect Eli. That was an unnecessary shot, and I had to let him know about it."

The Giants rarely hit back. Manning said his team "just couldn't get anything going."

Coughlin said the offensive line "was completely outplayed" and Brandon Jacobs, who ran for only 21 yards, said the game was "the worst I've ever experienced in my seven years of playing here. We used to be in the top two, three in the league and now we're 40th. I got the ball and took what they gave me, there was nothing more than I could have done." ▪

Above: Brandon Jacobs carries the ball during the first quarter. Jacobs gained just 21 yards on the ground.
Opposite: Eli Manning throws a pass in the third quarter. The Giants quarterback completed 18 of 35 passes for 264 yards.
(N.Y. Post: Charles Wenzelberg)

REGULAR SEASON

NOVEMBER 28, 2011 | SAINTS 49, GIANTS 24

BLUE DAT!

Saints Deal Reeling Giants Third Straight Loss

By Paul Schwartz

Maybe the undefeated Packers will be so overconfident by what they watched last night that they sleep all week and don't bother to prepare at all for Sunday's game at MetLife Stadium. Even then it might not be a fair fight.

After seeing what Drew Brees did to a completely overwhelmed and uncompetitive Giants defense, you can just imagine what Aaron Rodgers is thinking as he loosens up his right arm.

The Giants talked a good game this past week, disgusted by their passive resistance in a 17-10 loss to the Eagles but their words rang hollow as they were outclassed on "Monday Night Football" by the high-flying Saints.

Brees was untouched and undeterred as he threw for 363 yards, fired four touchdown passes and ran for another touchdown inside the rocking Superdome as the Saints piled it on the hapless Giants in a 49-24 rout that isn't going to bode well for Tom Coughlin's ability to right the sinking ship and keep hold of his job for another season.

"I'm not worried about next week yet," Coughlin said. "This is going to be a very short week. It didn't start out the way we wanted it to, it would have been nice to go home with a win and have that no sleep Tuesday with a win under our belt. It didn't happen."

No it didn't happen. Not even close. The Giants were torched for 577 total yards, the second highest total allowed in franchise history. The Saints got two touchdown catches apiece from Jimmy Graham and Lance Moore and also rushed for 205 yards in about an abysmal defensive display as can be imagined. Inside the visitors' locker room, the Giants seemed less shocked than they were bewildered about what went on.

"It's unacceptable," safety Antrel Rolle said.

"In the passing game, they kinda did what they wanted to do," added defensive tackle Chris Canty.

If ownership is looking for fight, resolve and a strong finish, this wasn't the vision to inspire any notion at all that the Giants are headed anywhere but out of the playoffs for a third consecutive year. They were thoroughly outclassed by the Saints in every way, especially the way their uninspired defense was shredded and embarrassed by Brees and Co. Eli Manning threw for 406 yards and Victor Cruz had 157 receiving yards and two touchdowns, but it was like rolling a very large boulder up an extremely steep hill.

"We can't get down and we can't get frustrated. We have to figure out a way to bounce back," Manning said.

"We played hard, that's why it's so frustrating," added Justin Tuck. "You look at the score it looks like we laid down, but I didn't see that. I saw guys hustling, I saw guys fighting. We're going to keep swinging, we don't know how to quit."

The free-fall is now in full descent. With three consecutive

Coach Tom Coughlin and defensive end Justin Tuck look on from the sideline during the Saints' 49-24 win over the Giants. (AP Images)

losses, the Giants have dropped like a rock from the 6-2 perch they held at mid-season and they are on the outside looking in as far as playoff positioning.

The Giants (6-5) are now a full game behind the first-place Cowboys (7-4) in the NFC East and that one-game deficit could easily become a two-game gap by the time the Giants for the first time this season face the Cowboys Dec. 11 in Dallas. That's because the slumping Giants return home on Sunday to play the unbeaten Packers, while the surging Cowboys play at the 4-7 Cardinals.

This was more target practice than NFL competition for Brees. It actually was a moderately competitive situation late in

the first half, with the Giants trailing 14-3. It looked as if that's the way the Giants would sneak into halftime as Brees got the ball on his own 12-yard line with only 1:09 remaining in the half. It took Brees 34 seconds to move the Saints 88 yards in five plays, a rapid-fire drive started with a 50-yard pass to Marques Colston and ended with Brees tossing the second of two scoring passes to Lance Moore to make it 21-3.

"It was just from the beginning of the game, they executed and we got down in the tank," linebacker Mathias Kiwanuka said. "We can't do that. We got to be able to rise up after a team scores and play hard, play harder in fact. We just didn't do that." ▪

Above: Dejected players look on from the bench during the fourth quarter. The 25-point loss marked the Giants' worst performance of the season. Opposite: Saints tight end Jimmy Graham completes an 18-yard reception in the first quarter. Saints quarterback Drew Brees passed for four touchdowns in the win. (AP Images)

THE MAKING OF JPP

The Humble and Earnest Beginnings of Sudden Superstar Pierre-Paul

By George Willis

The neatly kept pink house on the corner of a quiet neighborhood just off I-95 near the Fort Lauderdale Airport shows no signs of the famous football player whose parents live there. Inside, Jean Pierre-Paul is sitting at a table chatting in Creole to his wife, Marie, about the events of the day as married couples do.

When a reporter knocks on the door, Marie answers through a window and asks in a soft, but assured voice what his purpose is. When told The Post wants to speak with the parents of Giants defensive end Jason Pierre-Paul, she cautiously opens the door and flashes the kind of smile that all proud mothers flash.

"That's my son," she says.

It's clear she is more agreeable to the interview and a few pictures than her husband Jean, who has been blind since Jason was eight months old. He is tall, fit and a man of strength, even without sight.

First, Marie must telephone her 24-year-old daughter, Nadie, to get assurance it is OK to be interviewed. Once an anonymous family simply trying to create their own American dream, the Pierre-Pauls are learning to live with not being so anonymous now that their son is in the Super Bowl.

"She says it's OK," Marie tells the reporter. "But I need to fix hair for pictures."

There was a time Jason hid his involvement in football from his mother because he knew she was against him playing the sport. But that time has passed. The Pierre-Pauls will be in Indianapolis next Sunday when the Giants play the Patriots in Super Bowl XLVI. It will be the first game in person Jean and Marie will see their son, nicknamed "JPP," play as a Giant.

"Everything is good," she says. "They're in the Super Bowl. They've done a good job."

The hullabaloo surrounding the Super Bowl is something Jean and Marie Pierre-Paul sense but is not that important to them. They are more about family than sports. It reflects in the home, which is warm and neat. But among the several photos adorning their living room, there is not a single picture of Jason in a Giants uniform.

Football is simply an occupation. Surviving is the ultimate victory.

Jean left the poverty and horrors of Haiti in 1983, landing in South Florida and taking whatever work he could find. He was eventually joined by his wife and oldest daughter three years later. Nadie, Jason and then Herbie were born in Deerfield Beach. But by then Jean's vision had gone from blurriness to being legally blind. Doctors never found a real reason why.

It became a family fight for survival. Marie worked as a

Jason Pierre-Paul recorded 16.5 sacks in his second NFL season. (N.Y. Post: Charles Wenzelberg)

maid and housekeeper, and when Jason was old enough he worked, too.

"I had a lot of different jobs," Jason Pierre-Paul said yesterday at the Giants training facility in East Rutherford. "We had bills to pay. My dad wasn't working, and it was tough for my mom. People were always raising the rent, so I had to work, too. Everybody in the house worked to pay the rent."

JPP was the only one in his family with a passion for sports, but even he knew nothing of the Super Bowl. His sport was basketball, or at least he thought it was until he met Manny Martin, the defensive coordinator at Deerfield Beach High School.

Until landing in Martin's geometry class his junior year, Pierre-Paul had no intention of playing football. Martin's arm twist was essentially this: "If you want to pass this class, you're going to play some football."

Pierre-Paul began practicing with the team that day, though his parents were the last to know. He already had injured his leg three times, the last coming his sophomore year when he landed awkwardly while dunking a basketball. Pierre-Paul feared his parents might not approve of him playing football.

"I had to hide it for a little bit because I knew my mom wasn't going to let me play it," Pierre-Paul said.

To this day, he calls his mother after games to reassure her that he's fine.

"He calls me and everything is OK," she said. "After game he calls. During [the] week he calls. Everything OK."

Jason figured this football thing might work during his junior year in high school when Deerfield reached the state championship game with future Michigan quarterback Denard Robinson as a teammate. But his focus wasn't always what it should have been. He missed summer practices because of work and he struggled academically, failing to pass the Florida Comprehensive Assessment Test to get a diploma.

"He graduated with a certificate of attendance," Martin said. "The means you basically went to school for 13 years and didn't get anything."

It was then Martin looked Jason Pierre-Paul in the eye and told him of his responsibility to himself and his family and the possibilities his talent could bring.

"If you ever get your head together and do what you need to do for the next three years, you'll be able to take care of your family for the rest of their lives," Martin told the youngster.

By the time Jason Pierre-Paul finished at Fort Scott (Kansas) Community College, he had earned the equivalent of his high school diploma and an associate degree. After one year at South Florida where he collected 16½ sacks, the Giants made him their first-round draft pick in 2010. In his second NFL season, he was named to the Pro Bowl after collecting 16½ sacks during the regular season.

"At South Florida, that's where it really clicked and I knew I had a chance of making it here," Pierre-Paul said. "I'm stable now and I can actually learn the defense and adjust. I don't have to worry about myself moving anywhere."

Pierre-Paul is the pride of Deerfield Beach High School these days, especially this week.

"He was a different kind of kid," said Vincent Tozzi, the athletic director at Deerfield, as he leans against the gate of Butler Stadium. "This was the kind of kid who had to work for everything he's got. It wasn't easy. Like a lot of kids he worked to support his family."

One of Pierre-Paul's teachers, Michelle Scott, described him this way: "He was humble and well mannered. He's a deserving young man. We're proud of him."

So is his former coach: "For these kids to get out of here, they just need an opportunity," Martin said. "That's what he had. He took my advice and focused and buckled down for those next years at Fort Scott, then South Florida and then the Giants. He just took it and ran away with it."

Pierre-Paul, who signed a five-year $20 million deal as a rookie, drove a 1996 Grand Marquis in high school. Now he rides a BMW 750, because "you have to do something for yourself." One of his first tasks after the Super Bowl is to buy his mother and father a new home.

"I want her to pick a house, but I need to see it," Pierre-Paul said. "She almost paid for a house but the house wasn't all that. She finally decided she didn't like it either because it didn't have a big master bedroom. I told her when I come down I'll pick the house, because if I pick the house I know it's going to be good and she'll like it."

Having his parents at the Super Bowl means a lot to Pierre-Paul, though he says his father won't like all of the noise.

"My mom and dad taught me a lot," he said. "They kept me out of trouble and told me to go a better route. They taught me how to be a man, basically. We moved from place to place and it was hard to adjust to different schools. But we made it."

All the way to the Super Bowl. ∎

Jason Pierre-Paul is all smiles during a January press conference at the Giants' practice facility. (N.Y. Post: Charles Wenzelberg)

REGULAR SEASON

DECEMBER 4, 2011 | PACKERS 38, GIANTS 35

PACKERS REMAIN PERFECT

Rodgers Turns Thriller into Eli & Co.'s 4th Straight Loss

By Paul Schwartz

The Giants went toe-to-toe with the mighty Packers and, after Eli Manning matched the otherworldly Aaron Rodgers with a late touchdown drive, it was 35-35 with 58 seconds left. If Manning and his mates could get their hands on the ball in overtime yesterday it sure appeared likely the Packers would be unbeaten no more and the Giants would have ignited their season with a titanic upset.

It was all right there for the Giants, but instead of soaring out of MetLife Stadium with a memorable victory, they were left to wonder if yet another loss can lead to something good as they wobble their way through a very bumpy descent down but not out of a playoff chase.

"Those guys are the champs, and you got to knock the champs out," Justin Tuck said. "I think we had 'em on the ropes and we let 'em off. They're the champs, they're gonna get every call. The ball's going to bounce their way, you got to outplay 'em. I think we played to a draw up until that last field goal. We got to knock 'em out."

The knockout was administered by Rodgers, who got the ball with 58 seconds left on his own 20-yard line. Four straight completions later, he set the table for Mason Crosby to nail a 31-yard field goal at the closing whistle. That sent the Giants to their fourth consecutive loss, this one an agonizing 38-35

setback that keeps the Packers undefeated and left the Giants, now 6-6, searching and hopeful that coming close will bode well for the stretch run.

"I am extremely proud," safety Antrel Rolle said. "We fought from the first whistle to the very end. Unfortunately we came up a little short, but it is fine because we will see them again."

See them again? On television?

Losing game after game is a funny way to get where you want to go but the Giants are still only one game out of first place in the NFC East, thanks to the Cardinals out in Glendale, Ariz., knocking off the Cowboys (7-5) 19-13 in overtime. The Giants, believe it or not, can move into first place on Sunday in Dallas when they play the first of two games with the Cowboys in the final month of the season.

"We have four games to go and three of them are in our division," coach Tom Coughlin said. "We have to regroup and I think this brings us together even tighter than we have ever been before as a team."

That might be a portent of things to come or merely wishful thinking. Coughlin and everyone else recalls the way the Giants fought and lost 38-35 to the unbeaten Patriots in the final game of the 2007 season and how that catapulted them into their historic postseason run. Now they are hoping a loss to an undefeated team by the exact same score produces similar results.

Packers linebacker Clay Matthews celebrates after tackling Eli Manning in the third quarter. (N.Y. Post: Charles Wenzelberg)

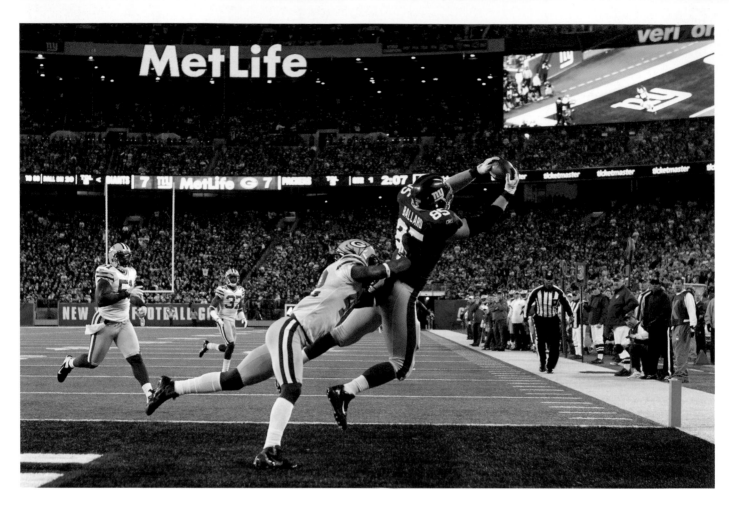

"You look at history and think it's going to repeat itself. We still got to come out and find that passion like we did in '07," Tuck said.

The Giants found the passion that was lacking in last week's 49-24 loss in New Orleans but they couldn't find their way to that elusive seventh win. Rodgers had his most mortal game of the season and still threw for 369 yards and four touchdowns.

Yet the Giants showed they mean business right away, with Manning finding tight end Travis Beckum on a 67-yard touchdown pass on the game's third play. Packers linebacker Clay Matthews intercepted and returned an awful Manning pass 38 yards for a score to put the Packers up 14-10. It was 21-17 Packers at halftime, but Rodgers hit Greg Jennings on a 20-yard scoring pass and the Giants were down 28-17 in the third quarter and in danger of losing touch.

Manning, though, feasted on Green Bay's suspect secondary and was aided by the return of Ahmad Bradshaw, which helped Brandon Jacobs get loose in the running game. Manning on a

fade to Hakeem Nicks got the Giants within 28-24 and a 50-yard field goal by Lawrence Tynes cut the deficit to 28-27 early in the fourth quarter.

Rodgers with 3:34 left hit Donald Driver to make it 35-27, but the Packers couldn't stop Manning, who was operating behind a revamped offensive line, with Kevin Boothe starting at center and Mitch Petrus making his starting debut at left guard. Manning finished off a 69-yard drive by drilling one into Nicks for a 2-yard scoring pass and on the all-important two-point conversion, D.J. Ware scored on an inside handoff to pull the Giants even at 35.

"They're the best team in football and we had them tied up with 58 seconds [left]," Manning said.

It wasn't tied for long and that Rodgers said "This was our toughest game of the season" didn't ease the sting. Or blunt the optimism.

"We're not out of the fight," Rolle said. "We're going to fight to get into these playoffs, and once we get into these playoffs, there's not going to be anything to stop us then." ▪

Above: Giants tight end Jake Ballard catches a pass in the end zone in the first quarter. Ballard was ruled out of bounds. Opposite: A dejected Eli Manning walks off the field following the Giants' fourth consecutive loss. (N.Y. Post: Charles Wenzelberg)

REGULAR SEASON

DECEMBER 11, 2012 | GIANTS 37, COWBOYS 34

MAGIC MANN!

Eli Leads 1st-Place Giants' Incredible Rally Past 'Boys

By Paul Schwartz

Maybe. Just maybe, the Giants have a season after all. Last night, they saved their absolute best for last in a thrilling, chilling 37-34 victory over the Cowboys, secured with one second left, by a fingertip.

Yes, by the fingertip of Jason Pierre-Paul, their wunderkind defensive end who somehow rose up and blocked Dan Bailey's 47-yard field goal attempt, the ball slamming to the turf at Cowboys Stadium with one second remaining, sending the Giants into a joyous celebration.

Before that, the Giants had trailed 34-22 with 5:41 remaining, but Eli Manning drove them back not once, but twice on clutch drives. The Giants got their winning points with just 46 seconds left on Brandon Jacobs' 1-yard touchdown run to make it 35-34 and a two-point conversion run by D.J. Ware to make it a three-point margin.

Incredibly, Tony Romo got the Cowboys to the brink of overtime. Two passes to Miles Austin put the Cowboys in position for Bailey. He calmly nailed a 47-yard field goal but, just before the snap, Giants coach Tom Coughlin used his last timeout to ice the rookie kicker. Given another chance, Bailey's kick was batted away by Pierre-Paul.

Despite going more than a month between victories, the Giants (7-6) have maintained what every team craves: control.

The Giants and Cowboys are now tied atop the NFC East, but the Giants hold the tiebreaker based on coming up big in this game.

The pathway to the playoffs is now clear for the Giants: win two of their last three games, just as long as one of those victories comes against the Cowboys on New Year's Day. The Giants face the Redskins (4-9) and the Jets (8-5) before meeting up again with the Cowboys in what could be a glorious way for them to ring in 2012.

This should quiet, at least for a week, the murmurs about Coughlin's job security as the Giants halted a four-game losing streak, a month's worth of losing that caused them to plummet from a commanding lead in the division.

All season, the Giants have alternated from poor to painful to amateurish in their pass coverage and that nearly did them in again. Rookie cornerback Prince Amukamara was exposed, getting beat twice deep by Laurent Robinson. The second was an absolute killer, as Romo ducked out of trouble and located Robinson running free, hitting him on a 74-yard catch and run with Amukamara trailing badly. On the next play, Romo hit Miles Austin on a 6-yard scoring pass to put the Cowboys ahead 27-22 with 12:43 left.

That was plenty of time for Manning. But his third-down pass intended to be a screen to Ware was deflected by Victor Butler

Eli Manning celebrates after the Giants scored a 2-point conversion to take a 37-34 lead late in the game.
(N.Y. Post: Charles Wenzelberg)

and intercepted by Sean Lee, who returned the ball to midfield.

Two plays later, Romo again slipped out of trouble, rolling to his right, a move that for some reason completely froze safety Antrel Rolle. He stopped running, leaving Dez Bryant embarrassingly alone. With cornerback Corey Webster giving chase but having no chance, Bryant walked into the end zone for a 50-yard touchdown with 5:41 left to make it a 34-22 Cowboys lead.

Manning hit Jake Ballard on an 8-yard touchdown pass with 3:14 remaining to make it 34-29. The only chance for a Giants comeback hinged on a defensive stop, and they got it with a three-and-out.

The Giants took over on their own 40-yard line with 2:12 remaining and one timeout to work with. Manning got the drive started with a 21-yard pass to Ballard and then fortune smiled. A high snap by center Kevin Boothe sailed over Manning, but a huge loss was negated by an offside penalty on DeMarcus Ware.

With 1:27 left, Mario Manningham dropped what should have been a 24-yard touchdown pass, but Manning remained undeterred. He again found Ballard, this time for 18 yards, the big tight end dragged down on the 1-yard line.

The Giants didn't rush things here. Jacobs was stopped for no gain and the Cowboys called their last timeout. On the next play, Jacobs got into the end zone, with 46 seconds left, his second score in a 19-carry, 101-yard night. ■

Above: Brandon Jacobs scores on a 1-yard run in the second quarter as the Giants took a 12-7 lead. Opposite: Jacobs hurdles over Cowboys defender Gerald Sensabaugh in the first quarter. The Giants running back gained 101 yards on 19 carries, scoring two touchdowns. (N.Y. Post: Charles Wenzelberg)

PIERRE-PAUL'S PLAY CARRIES DAY FOR GIANTS

BY MIKE VACCARO

In the middle of the scrum, in the rush of a moment, Jason Pierre-Paul figured he still had a full night's work ahead of him. He had tried once more to bull-rush the placekicker over one of the guards, and missed, and he had heard the crowd erupt.

"Overtime," he said to himself, figuring the delight of 95,952 people had to indicate Cowboys kicker Dan Bailey had drilled his 47-yard field goal, tied the game at 37, forced a little time-and-a-half on the Giants and the Cowboys.

Then, over the din, Pierre-Paul heard something else: the voice of referee Scott Green.

"Timeout, New York," Green said. "Third and final timeout."

And suddenly, a thought occurred to Jason Pierre-Paul:

"There's no reason we HAVE to have overtime."

Pierre-Paul had already had one of the greatest games of his two-year career. It had started with a sack of Tony Romo five minutes into the game that yielded two critical points when Romo wound up stumbling into the end zone for a safety. He added another sack later on. Just before halftime he had stripped Felix Jones of the ball, setting up a field goal.

"He's really something else," coach Tom Coughlin said later, smiling the kind of smile you rarely see from a head coach in December.

Timeout over, Pierre-Paul figured he would have to try something different. Time after time last night, he had come after Bailey from an angle. Now he would try something else. As the ball was snapped, Pierre-Paul came right up the gut, leaving tread marks on long snapper L.P. Ladouceur, raising his hands, together, over his head, as high as they would go....

"And then..." he said, extending his left hand, showing where football had collided with flesh, showing the place where the game had gone to die for the Cowboys, the place where the Giants' impossible 37-34 comeback for the ages had been etched into the books forever.

"I felt the ball hit my hand," Pierre-Paul said, "and I knew one thing: no overtime."

The Giants would have been buried long before if not for Pierre-Paul, who terrorized the Cowboys on one side of the ball, and Eli Manning, who tortured them on the other. The Cowboys had seized a 34-22 lead with six minutes left, mostly because, as dominant as Pierre-Paul had been, it's impossible for him to play safety, cornerback and nickel back, too.

Manning brought them back, throwing a touchdown pass to Jake Ballard, rushing them back down the field and handing off to Brandon Jacobs for the go-ahead score. A week ago, they discovered 58 seconds was too long to let an elite quarterback play with their fate; last night it was 46 seconds, and even if Tony Romo is no Aaron Rodgers, he was good enough to get the Cowboys within range a second week in a row.

Last week against the Cardinals in Phoenix, Bailey had made what looked to be a game-winning field goal in OT before he realized his own coach, Jason Garrett, had frozen him with a timeout.

This time it was Coughlin utilizing the more conventional strategy of icing the other guys' kicker.

And this time, it was Pierre-Paul who interceded the second time, not Bailey's own nerves. Pierre-Paul, who after the game had a humble message that ought to send shivers through the rest of the NFC.

"I'm still learning," he said. "There's still so much more I can do better, so much more I can do to help this team."

He is a young defensive lineman on the Giants, which means he has one of the best internships in football, with Jason Tuck and Osi Umenyiora offering daily advice and alums like Michael Strahan on call for occasional seminars.

"No place better to learn what I want to learn," he said.

And no time better to put all of it into practice than last night, fourth quarter, a season hanging in the balance and a football zooming straight for him.

"We needed to have a little celebration," Coughlin said. "We'd been starving."

The kid lineman picked up the tab, and picked up his teammates, too. Something else. ∎

Jason Pierre-Paul goes airborne to block Dan Bailey's game-tying field goal attempt in the fourth quarter, sealing the Giants' win over their division rival. (N.Y. Post: Charles Wenzelberg)

REGULAR SEASON
DECEMBER 18, 2011 | REDSKINS 23, GIANTS 10

GIANTS LEFT RED'-FACED

Big Blue Drops the Ball, but Still Controls Playoff Destiny
By Paul Schwartz

The Giants yesterday finally avoided playing a close game that took them down to the frantic closing seconds.

They ditched the late dramatics in a startlingly effective way: They barely played at all.

"I can't say it any more bluntly," a subdued Tom Coughlin said after the carnage. "I expected more."

He could not have gotten less.

Beaten on the ground, in the air, early, often and on first, second and third downs by the going-nowhere Redskins, the Giants yesterday spread some holiday jeer to their groaning and increasingly underwhelmed fans. They displayed many of their trademark defensive lapses and added in a new wrinkle of shoddy play by Eli Manning and his receivers, a combination that led to a desultory and numbing 23-10 loss that was never close but actually does not kill off their playoff aspirations.

"We looked like the four-win team out there today, rather than the Redskins," defensive tackle Chris Canty said. "It's embarrassing. I'm embarrassed."

This was beyond embarrassing. Manning threw three interceptions and the defense for the second time this season made Rex Grossman look like a winner. The Giants trailed 17-0 in the second quarter, 17-3 at halftime, 23-3 in the fourth quarter and did not get their first and only touchdown until

33 seconds remained, with the empty gray seats at deserted MetLife Stadium serving as witnesses to this football crime.

"I've got a big knot in my stomach for the way we just played," Justin Tuck said.

As sick as they looked, their postseason chances did not expire. The Giants (7-7), losers of five of their last six games, are now one full game behind the Cowboys (8-6) but still have control of their playoff destiny. On Christmas Eve, they can be eliminated from playoff contention if they lose to the Jets and the Cowboys beat the Eagles. That would create a two-game gap and make the Giants-Cowboys regular-season finale on New Year's Day meaningless.

But despite not at all looking like a playoff team, the Giants will be one if they win their last two games. If they win out, they will be 9-7 and the NFC East champs, because they will have beaten the Cowboys twice. The possibility remains for a three-team gridlock with the Giants, Cowboys and Eagles all owning records of 8-8, the Eagles will win the tiebreakers and the Dream Team will move on.

The loss, though, did eliminate the Giants from the wild-card picture.

Of course, linking the Giants and the playoffs could be seen as blasphemous. They performed as if they had nothing to play

for, which was the case for the Redskins (5-9) except no one told the Redskins.

"We just didn't have enough fight throughout the entire game," said safety Antrel Rolle, who offered several theories but not many solutions as to the plight of the Giants. "It's football, man. If you don't have enough fight, then you don't deserve to be on the field."

Rolle said he believes the Giants have heart but, "Honestly I don't know why we don't go out and display it every game." He also went on a riff about players needing to practice despite "nicks and bruises."

After the season-opening loss to the Redskins Rolle said the Giants would beat them 95 out of 100 times. If that's the case, the Giants had better win 95 of the next 98 games because the Redskins are 2-0 on them this season.

"We're 10 times better than what we showed out on the field today," Rolle said. "I don't know, man."

Nothing worked for the Giants. Manning misfired on his first six passes. The Giants intercepted two of Grossman's passes in the first quarter and got nothing out of it. Hakeem Nicks dropped what should have been a 54-yard touchdown pass. Rookie cornerback Prince Amukamara was so tentative in coverage that he was benched in the second half. Coughlin challenged a ruling and lost — the seventh consecutive lost challenge by Coughlin, once the king of challenges.

"They played better than us, that's what it came down to," understated Manning.

"It's shocking, it [stinks], it's tough to swallow," added Mathias Kiwanuka. "You never see something like this coming."

What's coming next is a battle with the Jets, who yesterday were hammered in Philadelphia. The winner lives on, the loser is in big trouble.

"I'm not worried," Rolle said. "When it slips away I'll just say it slips away. Hopefully it doesn't get to that point. I'm not worried because I'm very confident in our team." ■

Victor Cruz cannot come up with a pass in the first quarter. The Giants offense struggled to score against the last-place Redskins, falling to Washington for the second time in 2011. (N.Y. Post: Charles Wenzelberg)

REGULAR SEASON

DECEMBER 24, 2011 | GIANTS 29, JETS 14

HOLIDAY JEERS

Big Blue a Win from Playoffs; Jets on Life Support

By Brian Costello

The Giants delivered a gift-wrapped message to Jets coach Rex Ryan yesterday — stuff a stocking in it.

Big Blue took the "Battle of New York" with a convincing 29-14 victory over the Jets in front of 79,088 fans at MetLife Stadium, keeping their playoff hopes alive and dealing the Jets a virtual death-blow.

If that wasn't enough to shut up Ryan, Giants running back Brandon Jacobs personally delivered the message when the two had an on-field confrontation after the game. Jacobs and Ryan had to be separated with the two shouting obscenities at each other.

"Rex Ryan is a very disrespectful bastard," Jacobs said on ESPN. He later called him a "big-mouthed" and "big-bellied" coach.

Ryan declined to fire back, saying it was a "private conversation" and he did not care about Jacobs.

It was a fitting end to a crazy week for New York football. The two teams exchanged words all week through the media. The Giants arrived at MetLife Stadium yesterday for a Jets "home" game to find the paintings of their logos and the logos of their Super Bowls covered with black curtains. The Giants later ripped the curtains down.

"They've got to be quiet as far as whose stadium it is and all that other [junk] and garbage," said Giants defensive tackle Chris Canty, who sacked Mark Sanchez in the end zone for a safety in the fourth quarter that ended the Jets' hopes. "We came in here, they wanted to make a big deal about that, but we won this football game."

The Giants (8-7) now control their playoff fate. Beat the Cowboys next week and they win the NFC East. For the Jets (8-7), it's a lot more complicated. They need to beat the Dolphins then get losses from the Bengals and Titans plus a loss from either the Raiders or Broncos.

With the Jets playoff hopes looking dim, Ryan had to concede the Giants are a better team than his Jets. "They were definitely the better team today, the better team this year," Ryan said. "Clearly, I was wrong. I'll take the responsibility. It's on my shoulders, and it should be."

Giants coach Tom Coughlin declined the chance to take some shots at the brash Ryan.

"We won the game, that's the message," the tight-lipped coach said.

Giants owner John Mara admitted this victory was a little sweeter than most.

"Given everything that was at stake, given all the noise that's been coming out of Florham Park, yeah, it means a little more," Mara said.

Will this shut Ryan up?

"I know we won the game," guard Chris Snee said. "I don't care, they can talk, I'm sure they still are. We won the football game, they lost."

Early on, it looked like the Jets would control the game. They scored on their first possession and the Giants offense looked helpless. The game completely changed just before halftime.

Linval Joseph and the rest of the Giants defense harried Mark Sanchez into making four fourth-quarter miscues—two interceptions, a fumble, and a safety—and sealed the 29-4 victory over the Jets. (N.Y. Post: Charles Wenzelberg)

Trailing 7-3, the Giants were pinned at their own 1. On third-and-10, Eli Manning hit Victor Cruz with a 10-yard pass outside the numbers that Cruz turned into a 99-yard touchdown, racing past the Jets defenders. That gave the Giants a 10-7 lead at half-time, despite gaining just 83 yards other than that play.

Manning completed just nine passes in the game, but that was enough.

The Giants pushed the lead to 17-7 at the end of the third quarter on a 14-yard touchdown run by Ahmad Bradshaw, where he ran over Jets safety Brodney Pool.

The Jets defense gave the team chances to win in the fourth quarter, but Sanchez blew most of them. He had two interceptions and a fumble in the final quarter.

"I've got to get the ball to Mark," said center Nick Mangold. "I didn't, so I failed."

Sanchez said it wasn't that simple.

"That's really on both of us," he said. "That can't happen in a crucial situation like that. We had a good opportunity to score. We really let one go there on the goal line."

Sanchez had two other plays that were called fumbles on the field, and then overturned after being reviewed.

The Jets defenders were clearly annoyed with the offense's failures, but did their best not to outwardly rip Sanchez.

"Defensively we fought our [butt] off," linebacker Calvin Pace said. "Without trying to throw people under the bus, we lost by the same formula we always lose — penalties, turnovers, big plays.... It's the same [junk] every week."

The Jets still were in the game with 7:24 left when Sanchez ran in from the 1 to cut the Giants' lead to 20-14. The Jets had gotten the ball back when David Harris intercepted Manning on a surprising pass play by the Giants. They got the ball again with 5:39 left and down by six but went three and out on three straight passes, the final a sack. The Giants sacked Sanchez five times in the game.

The Jets got the ball back again with 2:24 left at their own 8 when Canty sacked Sanchez for a safety tomake it 22-14 and end the Jets' hopes. They tried an onside punt on the free kick but the Giants recovered, and Bradshaw scored on the Giants' first play from 19 yards out to ice the game.

With the game won, Jacobs made sure Ryan got the message Ryan and Jacobs had to be separated as they jawed at each other.

"We knew that's what we were going to get," Jacobs said. "We knew that's what we were going to get as soon as he had an opportunity to run his big, fat mouth. We knew that." ▪

Above: Ahmad Bradshaw powered into the end zone from 14 yards out late in the third quarter to give the Giants a 17-7 lead.
Opposite: Justin Tuck tallied four tackles and a sack as the Giants D dominated their New York rivals. (N.Y. Post: Charles Wenzelberg)

JACOBS TO REX: SCROOGE YOU

BY STEVE SERBY

Talk Is Cheap, Play the Game took an unexpected and vicious holiday the minute Giants 29, Jets 14 ended yesterday. That was when Brandon Jacobs became the mouth that roared back at Rex Ryan.

"Rex Ryan is a disrespectful bastard," Jacobs said to ESPN, later adding, "The Jets have a big-mouthed, big-bellied coach that talks too much."

All the animosity and bad will Ryan has spread across Big Blue Nation over the past three years was shoved back in Ryan's face both on the field and after the game by the lead bully of a Giants team that bullied Mark Sanchez and the Jets — their little brother Jets — and kept their NFC title hopes alive with the Cowboys showdown looming a week from today.

Jacobs' message for Ryan?

"You need to shut up," Jacobs said. "He's a great coach, and I take nothing away from him. Comes from a great coaching family, but he just needs to shut up."

That was Jacobs' message delivered through the media. On the field after the Battle of New York, Jacobs delivered his message in person.

"Well you know I didn't really say too much to him," Jacobs said.

"I know he told me, 'Shut the F up. Wait 'til we win the Super Bowl.'

"And I told him I'll punch him in his face."

Jacobs was asked if he had said something to Ryan prior to that exchange.

"I told him out of all of these Giant players on this football team, you're talking to the wrong one," Jacobs said.

Was that the first part of the conversation?

"I wasn't talking to him.... He just came out of nowhere and started at me," Jacobs said. "It was a great win for us. I don't want to harp on that.

"We're gonna celebrate this win, and I'm gonna let him have the worst Christmas he can have."

Jacobs said that Ryan went after him "the way his pops [Buddy] went after [Kevin] Gilbride. And ran afterwards."

Jacobs was informed Ryan had admitted he was wrong and conceded the Giants were the better team.

"He woke up the morning after their game last week knowing that," Jacobs said. "He just felt that he needed to give himself and his team some confidence. That's all."

Ryan's reaction to the rift?

"We had a private conversation. That's all I'll leave it as. Whatever. He doesn't like me. I respect him but I could care less about him."

Jacobs then bowled over Jets fans.

"I think we had more fans in the stadium than they did, and that's the way it was supposed to be because it's Giants Stadium... aka MetLife stadium," Jacobs said.

Jacobs was thrilled the Jets were on the schedule at the perfect time.

"I'm glad we had we had the Jets after the loss that we had against Washington," he said. "I knew that they were gonna fold, no matter what, to be honest with you, the way they been playing. And who am I to talk about the way they've been playing? We haven't played great. But I knew that they were gonna be the ones to crack because as far as them as an offense, I don't think they have what it took to beat us."

Jacobs was asked about the level of disrespect the Giants felt from Ryan. "We didn't really pay attention to it, to be honest with you, 'cause we knew that's what we were gonna get.... No matter what happened, we knew that's what we were gonna get as soon as he had an opportunity to run his big fat mouth. We knew that."

Does this validate the way Tom Coughlin goes about his business?

"Shut up and play," Jacobs said. "And that's what he tells us and that's what he's still trying to get across to me." ■

Brandon Jacobs, who had a solid day against the Jets with 42 yards rushing on seven carries, celebrates after fellow running back Ahmad Bradshaw's third-quarter touchdown run. (N.Y. Post: Charles Wenzelberg)

REGULAR SEASON

JANUARY 1, 2012 | GIANTS 31, COWBOYS 14

GIANTS FINISH THE JOB

East Champs Boot 'Boys to Set Up Falcons Battle

By Paul Schwartz

The word ringing through the ears of the Giants all season was a reminder of what they could not do last season: Finish.

There were so many times when it appeared as if the Giants were incapable of finishing. Last night, though, they finally cashed in on the marching orders presented to them by Tom Coughlin, the head coach who will be back at the helm again in 2012.

"We finished the game the way we wanted to finish it," Coughlin said. "We finished the regular season the way we wanted to finish it."

Faced with a regular-season-ending win-and-in, lose-and-out game against the rival Cowboys, the Giants started with a fury, withstood some tense moments and finished off the 'Boys with a flourish in a 31-14 victory before a roaring, towel-waving crowd of 81,077 at MetLife Stadium.

"The last couple of weeks, it's basically been win or go home," general manager Jerry Reese said. "You can call it the playoffs if you want to. Now it's the real playoffs. We're raring to go."

The record may be a modest 9-7, but as the NFC East champions the Giants get to stay home for the start of the playoffs and will face the wild-card Falcons (10-6) on Sunday at 1 p.m. at MetLife Stadium. Judging from the way the Giants blasted the

Jets last week and flicked away the Cowboys, there's a growing feeling now that they're in, the Giants just might stay awhile.

"I think we're in the perfect position," linebacker Mathias Kiwanuka said. "We didn't get here the way that we wanted to, but regardless of what has happened during the season we're in the playoffs, we won our division and we have a chance at the Super Bowl. Once you're in, the slate's wiped clean and this team is ready to play."

The Giants were certainly ready to play against the Cowboys, who head back to Dallas done at 8-8.

The resurgent Giants completely dominated for long stretches and surged to a 21-0 halftime lead, thanks to another hard-to-believe 74-yard catch-and-run from an extremely sharp Eli Manning to Victor Cruz. After two Tony Romo touchdown passes to Laurent Robinson closed the lead to 21-14 and an uneasy feeling of possible collapse in the damp air, the Giants closed things out in style.

"It's always got to be interesting with us," right guard Chris Snee said. "If we come out and play with the energy we did tonight, we can play with anyone."

It was Cruz who helped blunt the Cowboys' momentum with a 44-yard reception, simply outmuscling cornerback Orlando Scandrick for the ball at the Dallas 28-yard line on a third-

---

Eli Manning celebrates after Victor Cruz turned a short pass into a 74-yard touchdown to open the scoring against the Cowboys. The Giants were up by three touchdowns before Dallas scored, and they cruised to a 31-14 victory. (N.Y. Post: Charles Wenzelberg)

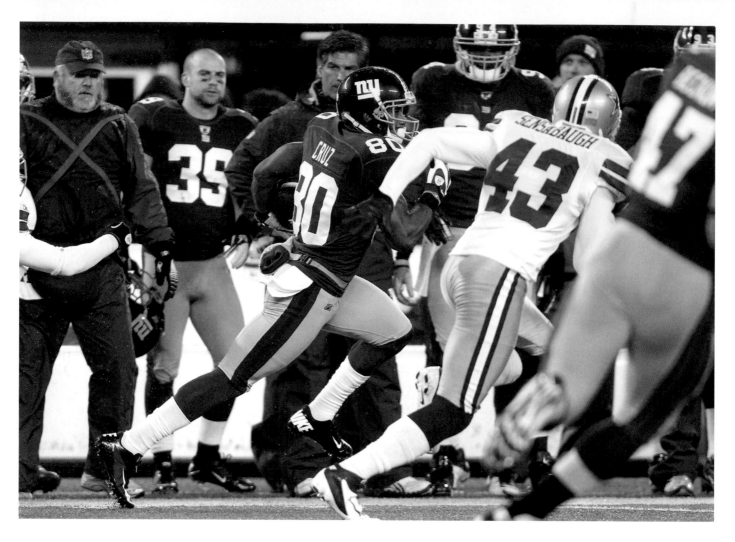

and-7 heave from an under-pressure Manning. That led to a Lawrence Tynes 28-yard field goal and a 24-14 Giants lead with 5:45 remaining. Chris Canty then got the fifth of the six sacks registered by a defense that welcomed back pass-rusher Osi Umenyiora, who after missing the past four games was right back in form with two sacks. A 36-yard pass to Hakeem Nicks set up Manning's 4-yard scoring pass to Nicks with 3:41 left, and it was party time for the Giants.

"That was nothing," said second-year defensive end Jason Pierre-Paul, who had one sack to give him 16½ this season. "Next week is going to be even better. We're in the playoffs!"

Romo, playing with a bruised hand, wasn't bad at all but he was hounded by the Giants up front and could not stand up to Manning, who compiled a passing rating of 136.7 after throwing for 346 yards with three touchdowns and no interceptions.

"Eli came through big-time," Coughlin said.

The Giants sprinted off the field at the break with their feet barely hitting the turf after putting together their most complete half of the season.

After Bear Pascoe kept a drive alive by leaping over cornerback Terence Newman for a first down, Manning threw short to Cruz for on a third-and-one for a first down — and more. Much more. Cruz ran past Newman and then past Gerald Sensabaugh, getting some room when Hakeem Nicks picked off cornerback Mike Jenkins. Cruz was gone from there, completing a 74-yard catch-and-run for a touchdown, and salsa dance, to make it 70.

Ahmad Bradshaw got the next two touchdowns and the Giants were on their way.

"We're a good football team," Umenyiora said. "We have a very good offense with an outstanding quarterback and as long as we're able to keep us in the game I think we'll have a chance to do something special." ▪

Above: Victor Cruz's first-quarter catch-and-run score was the big highlight, but the receiver hauled in six passes for 178 yards against Dallas. Opposite: A focused Eli Manning scorched the Cowboys defense, completing 24 of 33 passes for 346 yards, three touchdowns and no interceptions. (N.Y. Post: Charles Wenzelberg)

NFC WILD CARD PLAYOFFS

JANUARY 8, 2012 | GIANTS 24, FALCONS 2

GIANTS MAKE A STATEMENT

Pierre-Paul guarantees win over Packers

By Paul Schwartz

You cannot hold back the surging tide and you cannot hold back the living, breathing force that is the Giants when Eli Manning is passing with precision and especially when their defense reaches back to the halcyon days and treats an opponent with dominating disdain.

Don't even try to hold back the Giants when they finally get their dormant running game in gear, when they shrug off a slow offensive start with a fast finish, when they treat their towel-waving fans to a near-perfect 60 minutes of pressure-filled defensive excellence.

No sense going anywhere but with the flow of momentum that carried the Giants to a resounding 24-2 annihilation of the overmatched Falcons at roaring MetLife Stadium, a flow that carries the Giants out of the wildcard playoff round and into an NFC divisional game Sunday in Green Bay, where the Super Bowl champion and 15-1 Packers will be waiting.

"We're going to win," said Jason Pierre-Paul, the second-year defensive end/man-child who had another one of his punishing performances. "One hundred percent we're going to win...because we're the best."

Of course, the Packers until proven otherwise are the best, but the Giants are certainly peaking at the right time and have that interesting and last-second 38-35 loss to the Packers back on Dec. 4 still rattling around their brains.

"They're a good team. I think we have a very capable defense. It's gonna be a very, very good game," Osi Umenyiora said. "We're not going to go down there and lay down, we're going to go down there and fight."

Packers receiver Greg Jennings, not long after the Giants put the finishing touches on their masterful effort, tweeted "The team that kept us from our potential Super Bowl in '08 is back on OUR turf now. Trust me, we haven't forgotten."

The Falcons are not the Packers, not by a long shot, but they do possess weapons and the Giants trashed every one of them, wore down Atlanta's fast but smallish defense and turned a 7-2 halftime lead into a rout. And Manning threw three touchdown passes — two to Hakeem Nicks — and the defense was lathered up into a relentless fury.

"If we can continue to play defense like that, we can make ourselves heard in this tournament," said Tom Coughlin, who gained his first home playoff victory in his third try.

"We'll take the wins any way we can get 'em. It's not a template how you win games, but this is Giants football," added general manager Jerry Reese. "This is how we like to win games, we like to run the ball and play-action pass and play good defense."

It wasn't that long ago when the Giants defense was a complete mess, the unquestioned Achilles heel threatening to compromise all the exploits Manning was achieving. That time

Hakeem Nicks stepped up when the Falcons decided to blanket Victor Cruz. His four-yard grab for a score in the second quarter was just one highlight from a six-catch, 115-yard, two-touchdown day. (N.Y. Post: Charles Wenzelberg)

is gone. This was a complete shutout, with the only Falcons points coming on a second-quarter safety when Manning was called for intentionally grounding in the end zone. That put the Falcons up 2-0.

"Our defense was tremendous.... We should feel bad for giving them those two points," guard Chris Snee said.

They'll all get over it. The first order of business was containing running back Michael Turner and it was accomplished with stunning force; Turner was limited to 41 rushing yards on 15 carries. Matt Ryan was sacked twice and harassed far more often, never comfortable looking downfield as Julio Jones, Roddy White and tight end Tony Gonzalez made short-gain catches with little impact.

The Falcons managed a meager 247 total yards. Twice they tried Ryan on quarterback sneaks on fourth-and-1 and twice, as Osi Umenyiora said, the Giants "mushed him back."

It was defense all day for the Giants, holding down the fort until Manning and the offense shook off the cobwebs of a rough first half to take total command in the second. The Falcons made sure not to allow Victor Cruz to beat them and so Nicks did, getting the first Giants touchdown on a reach-back 4-yard scoring catch and electrifying the crowd and his team with a 72-yard

catch and run to make it 17-2 late in the third quarter. Mario Manningham, held without a catch last week, arose from his slumber with a 27-yard touchdown reception with 9:55 remaining to finish off the Falcons.

Manning actually had a 14-yard scramble to help set up the first touchdown and could at times lean on a rushing attack that came up with 172 yards — a full 50 yards higher than their best output in any game this season. The Giants had two runs all season of 30 or more yards and Brandon Jacobs and Ahmad Bradshaw each had one at least that long.

"We feel as tough as any NFL team in the league," Bradshaw said.

That toughness will surely be challenged this weekend. The early forecast in Green Bay for Sunday is 21 degrees and a possibility of snow.

"That's tropical" said Justin Tuck, thinking back on the frigid minus-23 degrees the Giants overcame in the 2007 NFC title game.

"I don't think they think 'The Giants are coming to kill us' or anything like that," Umenyiora said. "They're probably thinking they're going to win again and if I was them I'd be thinking the same thing. Hopefully we go out there and have a chance to shock the world." ■

Above: Eli Manning scrambles for 14 yards in the second quarter to set up the Giants' first touchdown. Opposite: Hakeem Nicks celebrates his 74-yard touchdown catch, but he must have felt just as good about a Giants D that yielded no points to the Falcons. (N.Y. Post: Charles Wenzelberg)

G-MEN PUT OLD-SCHOOL BRUISING ON SPLATLANTA

BY STEVE SERBY

They reached back deep into a violent past, when merciless merchants of mayhem like Sam Huff and Andy Robustelli and later Lawrence Taylor and Harry Carson and Michael Strahan defined what New York Football Giants was supposed to mean, and suddenly they are champing at the bit to march onto the tundra of Lambeau Field Sunday, be it frozen or not, and rip the Lombardi Trophy from the clutches of Aaron Rodgers and the Packers.

"You know the names, you know the history of what this team has been built on.... I think it brought back a lot of memories today how we played," Justin Tuck said after Giants 24, Falcons 2.

And now they believe in a way they have not believed in four years. They have believed in Eli Manning all season long, and now they have reason to believe in their running game and even better, a defense that fears no one and nothing, anywhere or anytime.

Big Blue's strangulation yesterday of Matt Ryan and Michael Turner was so bloodcurdling that less than half an hour after Splatlanta, monster Jason Pierre-Paul was all but doing a MetLife Leap from here to Titletown, U.S.A., when he announced: "We're gonna win."

Rodgers crushed the Giants' playoff dreams last December when he threw for 404 yards and four touchdowns in a 45-17 drubbing. He threw for 369 yards and four more touchdowns, with one interception, in the Packers' 38-35 victory at MetLife Stadium on December 4.

"He's played at a high level for a couple of years now, so we got our work cut out for us but," Osi Umenyiora said, "they got their work cut out for them also, because we're not any slouches. We're gonna go out there and we're gonna try to hit them in the mouth, and we'll see what happens."

Champing at the bit to shock the world again.

"We've earned the right to be able to do that," Chris Canty said. "I'm excited about how good this football team can be."

It won't be as cold as it was in the 2007 NFC Championship overtime game when Plaxico Burress willed his way through the pain and Corey Webster intercepted Brett Favre and Lawrence Tynes redeemed himself and booted the Giants to Super Bowl XLII, but Big Blue will show up every bit as cold-blooded.

"Pressure on the quarterback," Umenyiora said. "I think that's pretty much the only way you can beat Green Bay. Our offense continues to play well, and we force 'em in a situation where all they do is throw the ball, then I think we'll be able to be successful."

This is clearly a different Giants defense than the one Rodgers carved up at the end in their last meeting.

"It's the same team, but it's a different mentality, so we're ready to go," Mathias Kiwanuka said.

A Pack mentality.

"It's a playoff mentality," Kiwanuka said.

The Giants are bullies again, from Brandon Jacobs and Ahmad Bradshaw punishing defenders, to Canty defying and denying the Falcons twice on fourth-and-inches with his giant heart, to Pierre-Paul and Umenyiora and Tuck and Dave Tollefson and yes, Rocky Bernard, making life miserable on

the quarterback and easy on the defensive backs.

"It's just a fun time to be playing defense for the New York Giants," Tollefson said.

Big Blue was Bill Parcells-tough, and Bill Belichick-cerebral. Eleven angry men playing as one again. Relentlessness upfront, and relentless communication in the back end. Perry Fewell's finest hour.

I informed Tuck of Rodgers' eight touchdowns and 773 passing yards in the last two games against Big Blue.

"I don't know if it's too much of a concern," Tuck said. "We know he's a good quarterback, we know he's gonna get his numbers, but we just gotta do a good job of just keeping him rattled, keeping a lot of pressure on him and not give him the time."

What's the level of confidence?

"High," Tuck said. "High. Put that in capital letters."

HIGH. ∎

Chris Canty (99) and Aaron Ross (31) team up to manhandle the Falcons' Michael Turner in the first quarter, setting the tone for a Wild Card game that was controlled by a stifling Giants defense. (N.Y. Post: Charles Wenzelberg)

NFC DIVISIONAL PLAYOFFS

JANUARY 15, 2012 | GIANTS 37, PACKERS 20

LAMBEAU FEAT

Nicks' Hail Mary Fuels Another Big Blue Playoff Shocker in Green Bay

By Paul Schwartz

Sometimes, Osi Umenyiora said, "there's just a certain feeling you get."

The feeling coming into this game was overpowering, almost intoxicating.

"Honestly, I'm not just talking here, we came into this game really feeling like we were gonna beat them down," Umenyiora said. "I don't know why, I don't know what gave us that impression, but we just really thought we were gonna beat them. And we went out there and did it."

The Giants last night did not merely beat the Packers.

"No, we thought we were gonna beat them down," he stressed. "That's not to disrespect them or anything like that. There's just a certain feeling you get sometimes when you're going into a game."

The feeling overcoming the Giants nowadays is that they cannot be stopped. They are one game away from a second Super Bowl appearance in the past four years because they took the battle to the mighty Packers, invading Lambeau Field like marauders ransacking this famed football castle.

Eli Manning badly out-played the great Aaron Rodgers and completed a hard-to-fathom Hail Mary to Hakeem Nicks on the last play of the first half for a momentum-building touchdown.

The absurdly surging Giants defense ground the vaunted Packers' passing attack into the frozen ground and a tight game became a runaway as the Giants cruised to a stunning 37-20 victory in a NFC divisional playoff upset.

"I think we're a dangerous team," a proud Tom Coughlin said.

He should know. This unlikely march moves onward. There's a trip to be made out west to San Francisco, where the resurgent 49ers will be waiting Sunday as 2½-point favorites in the NFC Championship Game for the right to go to Indianapolis to represent the conference in Super Bowl XLVI.

"We told you all, don't jump on the bandwagon now," Justin Tuck said. "This football team will be ready to play. We're gonna be hard to beat."

The last time the Giants played at Candlestick Park, on Nov. 13, a late rally fell short in a 27-20 loss that, to a man, the Giants hoped they could avenge sometime down the line.

"I'm going to go ahead and answer this for you: Do we feel we're gonna win in San Fran?" Tuck said. "Yes, we feel like we're gonna win in San Fran. Am I guaranteeing a win? No, I'm not."

Of course there are no guarantees but if the Giants (11-7) can do this to the defending Super Bowl champs, a team that went 15-1 in the regular season, whom can't they beat? The

Desmond Bishop and the Packers defense continually came up short against Eli Manning and the Giants offense in New York's 37-20 drubbing of the defending Super Bowl champs. (N.Y. Post: Charles Wenzelberg)

Giants wanted another shot at the Packers after a 38-35 loss during the season and the rematch was a resounding reversal of fortune.

"I'm not surprised," safety Antrel Rolle said. "I said we'll see 'em again, we saw 'em again, this is the outcome."

The Packers as the No. 1 seed, coming off a bye, never got in synch and Rodgers after a magnificent season never looked like himself. He had 20 incomplete passes.

"We made him not look like himself, man, just like we've been doing to the rest of these quarterbacks," Umenyiora said.

Incredibly, Rodgers' longest completion was a mere 21 yards.

"That's a good stat for this team, against that quarter-back, something for us to be proud of," linebacker Mathias Kiwanuka said.

The Giants never trailed. Nicks broke free on a 66-yard catch and run for a touchdown to give the Giants a 10-3 lead and it expanded to 20-10 at halftime when Manning and Nicks connected on "Flood Trip," which is what the Giants call their Hail Mary. This one, from 37 yards away, was completed when Nicks soared over Charles Woodson and Charlie Peprah in the end zone.

"Once I went up and got it, I looked around and it was exciting," Nicks said.

"It gave us all the momentum going into halftime," Manning said.

Unlike the epic 23-20 overtime thriller four years ago here in the NFC title game, the Giants this time around did not need any late heroics.

The Giants led 23-13 on Lawrence Tynes' third field goal and got the ball back when Kenny Phillips whacked Ryan Grant, forcing a fumble that Chase Blackburn recovered and returned 40 yards to the Green Bay 4-yard line. Manning hit Mario Manningham on the next play for a touchdown and a 30-13 lead.

Rodgers answered with a touchdown drive but Victor Cruz recovered the onside kick and the Giants tacked on another, with Brandon Jacobs running it in to send the Lambeau faithful headed for the exits.

"The Packers don't have anything to hang their heads about," Tuck said. "I just think it seems like our time." ■

Above: Hakeem Nicks broke free from Tramon Williams and raced for a 66-yard touchdown to give New York at 10-3 lead at the end of the first quarter. Opposite: Brandon Jacobs celebrates a resounding victory that sent the Giants to the NFC Championship Game in San Francisco. (N.Y. Post: Charles Wenzelberg)

AVALANCHE HEADING TO SAN FRANCISCO

BY MIKE VACCARO

Maybe it's time we halt the comparisons to January of 2008, as fun as that association is. Maybe it's time we remember the white knuckles that defined so much of that glorious ride, the comeback in Dallas, the overtime struggle in Green Bay, the palpitation parade that was the Super Bowl against New England.

That team was terrific, and it reached the ultimate plateau, and that is something this team in front of us still has to do. But even those 2007-08 Giants, as touched as they were by pixie dust, as skilled as they were in negotiating late-game minefields, only rarely approached what we have seen from these Giants the past four weeks.

"Everything is clicking," Osi Umenyiora said, "and when that happens, we are a pretty tough team to match up with."

Umenyiora and friends had just sent 72,808 Cheeseheads back into the cold Wisconsin night, had flattened the Packers 37-20 and been dominant doing it. In four straight weeks, four straight win-or-be-gone trials, the Giants have won by 15 points against the Jets, 17 against the Cowboys, 22 against the Falcons and now this, a 17-point creaming that felt like so much more.

This isn't just a team peaking at the proper moment; it's a snowball that has quickly and remarkably rolled into an avalanche. It's a quarterback who is clicking with his receivers and defensive linemen who are meshing with linebackers and defensive backs to rebuild and reload a unit on the fly that Aaron Rodgers himself would call "quick, hard and devastating."

It is a coach who is at his best in these very games, who took Green Bay's Mike McCarthy to school not only in building a game plan but executing it, then managing the game in front of him. And sure: If you want to call that Eli Manning-to-Hakeem Nicks rainbow just before the half "fluky" — as Rodgers did — you're allowed. Some used similar words not so long ago when another Eli parabola attached itself to David Tyree's helmet.

But you know what else that team was called eventually?

It was called champion. And if it's still too early to distribute that label for this team, it's never too early to identify if a team has the elements to make it happen. And after two playoff games and two virtual ones, this much is certain:

This team does.

"We know how to win in the playoffs," Justin Tuck would say, "and we know how to win on the road. We know what it takes to get where we want to get to."

Said Tom Coughlin: "Success breeds confidence."

There haven't been many teams more brimming with confidence than the '07 Patriots and the '11 Packers, a combined 33-1 when they were forced to collide with the Giants. Both teams were classic bullies, able to turn a 14-0 lead into 42-0 because of extraordinary talent and relentless ambition.

And both turned out to have glass jaws when the Giants hit them back.

In Super Bowl XLII, it manifested in an offensive line that all but vanished under the crush of a supersonic Giants pass rush, turning Tom Brady into Steve Grogan. And yesterday, it meant turning McCarthy into Rich Kotite, a panic-stricken mess, calling an inexplicable onsides kick in the second quarter, going for a fourth-and-five from the Giants' 39 with 13 minutes left in a one-touchdown game.

The Big, Bad Pats? The Big, Bad Pack?

Not so big after crashing into the Giants. Not so bad.

"We knew what we were up against," Coughlin would say, and you wonder if the Packers had any idea what they were up against. You wonder if the 49ers do, as they lie in wait in northern California, 21 years after the last time these franchises met for a berth in the Super Bowl.

The world expected a Saints-Packers shootout for the NFC title, football as pinball. They get Giants-Niners instead. Maybe the other two can play in a consolation game somewhere.

"It seems like the light went on a few weeks ago," a happy, hoarse John Mara said in the locker room, and he's right. The Giants started playing for their season four weeks ago, and damned if they are going to loosen their grip anytime soon. Too bad Sunday can't come tomorrow. ∎

Eli Manning and his receiving corps were impeccable against the Pack. The quarterback racked up 330 yards passing and threw for three scores. (N.Y. Post: Charles Wenzelberg)

BRANDON JACOBS

Steve Serby catches up with the Giants' veteran running back

Q: Describe your mentality on the field.

A: I'm a dog. I'm a beast. I take the streets to the football field, that's what I do. I play like I'm trying to stay out of jail, like I'm fighting for my life. I go out there and I play with a dog mentality, an assassin's mentality, basically.

Q: Do you expect all your Giants teammates to play that way tonight?

A: I definitely expect all my teammates to show up with that mentality, even if that's not your mentality, no question.

Q: You look inside your teammates' eyes before every game.

A: To make sure their pupils aren't dilating. The window of a man's soul is straight through his eyes. When some fighters are nervous, their pupils dilate really a lot. I've seen dilated pupils in some people's eyes. It doesn't take long to see.

Q: And when you see it?

A: That's one person I have to have a lot of enthusiasm with and make sure I get him up out of his nervousness.

Q: And how do you do that?

A: Go out there and do the best I can to knock somebody on their and set a tone. It's going to be like this all night. Join me.

Q: What are the favorite moments of your Giants career?

A: I'd say the first one would have to be breaking the touchdown record for the franchise [on Dec. 11 against the Cowboys].... The 74-yard touchdown versus Dallas two years ago.... And running over LaRon Landry in the open field.

Q: If you win tonight, where would that rank?

A: It'll rank really high, mainly because of what's at stake and who it is we're playing.

Q: How would you want MetLife Stadium to be tonight?

A: I want it to be very, very crazy. I want it to be bananas. The loudest thing I've ever heard in my life.

Q: Does your 4-year-old son Brayden get a kick that you're No. 27 of the New York Giants?

A: No, he doesn't care about that at all. He knows what I do. He knows my number. He's just a normal kid.

Q: Is he more similar to you or your wife (Kim)?

A: He's more similar to my wife. He looks like her. He's real nice. He has no bad bones in his body, very respectful kid. He's a great kid. He's definitely my favorite 4-year-old in the whole wide world. I get a thrill even thinking about it. He's just big like me.

Q: How big is he?

A: 65, 70 pounds.

Q: Is your younger son (Quinn) more like you?

A: Yeah, he's definitely like me, mean, got a temper, doesn't really care about too much. What he wants is what he wants.

Q: How has fatherhood changed you?

A: Some decisions I would have made without kids, I would never make them now.

Q: Why did you and Plaxico Burress click?

A: We're two of the same kind of people, to be honest. We had it rough growing up. He is somebody I understand. Not a lot of people understand him. And vice versa: Not a lot of people understand me. He understands me. We just became close. He's a good-natured cat, you know? And you can't find too many cats like that.

Q: Your running backs coach, Jerald Ingram, has been showing clips of some of the old-time greats. What did you observe about Jim Brown?

A: I just watched how tough he was, how hard he ran. He didn't care who was in his way.

Q: Is that the way you run?

A: Yeah, I don't care who's there, I just keep going.

Q: Who else have you watched?

A: O.J. Simpson, Earl Campbell, Gale Sayers.

Q: Who in your family was the most proud that you just received your sociology degree from Fairleigh Dickinson?

A: I'd say my wife was definitely the proudest person in the world. She has two degrees. She was happy I stayed with it.

Q: Why did it mean so much to you?

A: I was the first person in my family to have one.

Q: Did your wife encourage you?

A: It was definitely something I wanted to do for the sake of our kids to say I have one. But sometimes she would have to push me to finish it.

Q: What was it like when you brought the diploma home?

A: My mom, everybody there was yelling and screaming all over the place. It was a good time. With it being the holidays, it was extra special.

Q: Did your mom want you to play football?

A: She didn't care what I did. She wanted to make sure I did the right thing.

Q: There was a lot of crime in Napoleonville, La. Did sports save you?

A: No question, sports definitely saved me. I had a lot of opportunities to go in a different direction.

Q: Sum up what it's been like being a New York Giant.

A: It's been one of the most exciting highlights of my life. It gave me an opportunity to do what I love to do, and it's a great organization. I can't say enough good stuff about the Mara family and the Tisch family. I got a chance to be close to both families.

Q: Did you meet Wellington Mara?

A: I got a chance to meet him once. I went up to him and introduced myself to him. It was an honor to have a chance to meet a person with such a strong appearance. He did a lot for the National Football League, not to mention the New York Giants organization.

Q: Are you hopeful you can continue your Giants career?

A: Yes, if I can continue my career as a Giant, that would be another highlight. If not, I understand the business.

Q: Why do you want to stay with this franchise?

A: It's where I started. I like it here. My wife likes it here. My kids are settling in good. It's a great organization to play for. It's people that respect you and care about you as a person. The whole nine.

Q: Do you have a gut feeling what might happen?

A: No, I don't have any.

Q: But your teammates are optimistic. What do they tell you?

A: "You're straight. You're going to be here." They seem sure. But you never know. I tell them, "Time will tell."

Q: Jason Pierre-Paul?

A: He's a beast. He can be so much better than he is now. He can get faster, he can get stronger, even more of a ferocious attitude. He could be a monster no one in the National Football League has ever seen before.

Q: The key to the Cowboys game tonight.

A: We need to run the ball. That's exactly what we need.

Q: Can you envision a scenario tonight where you do not walk off the field a winner?

A: Not at all. I don't see one scenario. I know they're going to bring everything they got. I think we're going to do the same thing. I think our guys want it more. I think we got just what it takes to go out and get the job done.

Q&A

ANTREL ROLLE

Steve Serby talks with the Giants outspoken safety

Q: Describe the mentality of every Giants player on that field Sunday.
A: We are Giants. That's going to be our approach. I think right now, we have an identity. We have an identity of who we are. Not who we're trying to be, but who we are.

Q: When you say "We are Giants," what exactly does that mean to you when you say that?
A: When I say we are Giants, that's just like me saying no one can measure the heart and the fight that we have on this team. If we go out there and play the way we want to play, with full focus, we know we can't be denied.

Q: Can this Giants team make the kind of magical run to the Super Bowl the XLII Giants did?
A: I think if we go out there and we take it one play at a time — not only one game at a time, one play at a time, and play for that play that's in front of you right there at that moment— without a doubt. We have what it takes on this team to go out there and get it done without a doubt. You name it, we have what it takes. No matter what position it is, we have what it takes to get it done.... I've wanted things bad in my lifetime, especially playing football. But I think this year, I don't think I've ever wanted anything as bad as I want it this year.

Q: You want what bad?
A: This championship.

Q: Because of the talent that's here?
A: Yeah, it's just what I feel. I think it's also what I know we

can do. When we click...we're something to deal with. When we click, it's lights out. We're coming. And I still think we have a lot of good football left in us.

Q: Your message to Giants fans?
A: It's been a tough year, but we're peaking. We're peaking at the right time, and we're going to continue to peak. We're going to continue to get better week in and week out. We're not going to stop here. We need all their support, more than ever now, and we're going to give them something to cheer for each and every week.

Q: How are you a "dog" on the field?
A: When I say a dog, that means I'm ready for whatever... whenever...however...wherever it comes, I'm willing to take it on.... I never say no, no matter what it is.... I don't care if there's a 360-pound lineman comin' my way, I'm going to chop his (butt) down. I'll go out there and I'll throw everything I got in there.

Q: Are you fearless?
A: I'm fearless. Without a doubt. And when I'm on the field, if it's you and me in a battle? I'm going to win 90, you might win 10. That's the way I look at it.... My mom always tells me like, "Trel, you're too hard on yourself, you know sometimes they're going to catch a ball." Like no, hell no. Not on me.

Q: How sick to your stomach were you after the New Orleans game?
A: It's one thing to go against a team that is just that much better than you — and New Orleans is a great football team — but

we made them look 10 times better than what they really are. We didn't help ourselves at all — from technique, from assignment, to passion, to aggressiveness.

Q: How often have you addressed the defense this season?

A: A few times.... When I feel something, I feel it deep.... When I was in Arizona for a number of years, I really didn't expect us to win—even the year we went to the Super Bowl (XLIII). I knew we had a good team, but we had to really, really jell and focus and put our minds together and damn near almost play mistake-free football to get to where we had to get to. This team, the talent is through the roof, and that's what I know, and that's what I feel.... When there's moments we look like we don't even know what the hell we're doing, or we look like we're not even in the football game, that's what I have a problem with...I felt myself wanting it so bad, and wanting this team to jell and have that chemistry so bad to the point where this one game we played excellent, then this two games we take off.... You play against New England and then you come back and lose five out of the next six...that alone was driving me crazy.

Q: Did you talk to Justin Tuck after you told the media everybody should practice?

A: I went to Tuck and I said, "Cap, let me tell you something—don't let this media get in your head with this bull." I'm telling you exactly what I told him word for word. And I said, "If I have something to tell you, or if you have something to tell me, we're going to go tell each other." We don't bite our tongues. We have a great relationship. I didn't feel like anything I was saying was brutal. For one, I know my teammates, and I think they know me.

Q: What has the experience been like being a New York Giant?

A: The first year was rough for me. I didn't know how to deal with, for one, the coaching styles. I felt like you kind of lost your professionalism as far as you being you — just allowing you to be yourself. I felt like everyone had to be the same person, and that's never been a part of how I play the game. I've always played the game carefree. You had a lot of fun playing it, but at the same time I got the job done. In practice at Arizona I would always have a yellow shirt on underneath my pads, it was just a mind thing for me. Or I may have U.M. (Miami) socks on, it was just something that I've always done. Coming here you have to have certain things, you have to do this, you have to do that.... I wasn't fond of it. I didn't understand what's with all these little things that really has nothing to do with football?

Q: Did you have talks with Coach Coughlin about it?

A: Yeah. His ways were his ways. He wasn't going to change though, I knew that. That's why in the offseason, just sitting down with my mother ... obviously football for me last year wasn't fun. I was frustrated a lot of time. I felt like it took me out of my game. I let the little things around here, me being annoyed with certain situations, get the better of me.

Q: Did you get in trouble for saying on Miami radio that you wanted to play for (Jets coach) Rex Ryan?

A: I never said I want to play for Rex, they asked me, "Would you mind playing for a coach like that?" I was like, "You know, I wouldn't mind." And I was only saying that — not to put Coach Coughlin down or anything — but it just seemed like Rex was letting them be themselves. And that's what I had a problem with. And I felt like, OK, well Coach Coughlin wants everyone to act and be like this — well I'm like, I'm not this person.

Q: So how did you get that resolved?

A: The thing that had to change was me. I had a decision to make, and ask myself questions: Well, is this a great franchise? Yes it is. Do you have great coaches around you? Yes we do. Do we have great teammates? Do we have talented teammates? Yes. Do I love New York City? Yes I do. When I weighed out the pros and cons, I'm like, OK, well what really bothers me? When I weighed it out, it's little stuff that can aggravate you, only if you let it aggravate you. Not saying that I still don't feel what I feel, I just know how to deal with it a whole lot better.

Q: What did you mean when you said recently that you're not the easiest cookie?

A: I'm very easy to get along with. I think I get along with anyone and everyone.... But I also don't take bull from anyone. I don't take no [garbage] from anyone. The same way I give respect, I demand it.

Q: You're that way on the field and off the field, right?

A: Absolutely.

Q: I'm a tight end, I'm a running back.... Why should I fear Antrel Rolle on the field?

A: Because he doesn't have any fear in him. A lot of times I might be the smallest guy on the field at the time. It doesn't matter. My heart is the size of Texas, I don't back down from any opponent, and I'm coming. And I'm coming with a lot of force. And I'm bringing it with you when I come.

NFC CHAMPIONSHIP GAME
JANUARY 22, 2012 | GIANTS 20, 49ERS 17

CHAMPS!

Giants Win NFC Championship on OT Field Goal, Setting Up Super Bowl Rematch Vs. Patriots

By Paul Schwartz

On the road. In the NFC Championship Game. In overtime. The Patriots, already in, awaiting the winner. Harsh weather affecting every move. A draining, physical battle. A field goal to win it.

It was all so eerily familiar.

"Everything that happened is happening all over again, you understand?" Osi Umenyiora said.

It is not easy to understand what is going down with these Giants. What transpired four years ago was coming alive again last night as a brutal slugfest of a game, in the rain and wind, was nearing its climax as Lawrence Tynes lined up for a 31-yard field goal.

"The parallels of this season are really ironic," Tynes said. You think?

Tynes, after a timeout attempting to ice him, drilled the game-winner 7:54 into overtime, sending the Giants past the 49ers, 20-17, in an overtime throwback defensive battle at dripping-wet Candlestick Park. Just like he did four years ago in frigid Green Bay, in overtime, Tynes made the kick that allowed the upstart Giants to play on.

"I'm not surprised, I'm delighted, I'm excited," Tom Coughlin said. "At times, it was difficult to contain yourself."

The Giants leaped into the air, landing on the muddy grass as Tynes raced to his wife, Amanda, both of them "crying like babies."

The kick, and all the energy expended to outlast a ferocious 49ers defense that knocked resilient Eli Manning around like a rag doll, produced a glorious grand prize, sending the Giants to Super Bowl XLVI, where waiting for them in Indianapolis will be the Patriots in a rematch of the classic upset four years ago in Glendale, Ariz., where the Giants ended the Pats' perfect season with a stunning, last-second 17-14 triumph.

Four years later, with 15 players from that title team sprinkling the roster with big-game experience, the Giants again take aim at Tom Brady and Co.

"It is hard to believe," co-owner John Mara said. "I think it will be a great game. I think there will be some points scored."

If so, it will be a stark contrast to what Coughlin called "just a classic football game" that featured "football at its most basic element." At times, it appeared as if no team could muster enough yards to get any more points and it was clear something unexpected was going to make the difference.

Unable to get anything accomplished with Manning in a collapsing pocket, the Giants were saved by a monstrously big

Eli Manning launches a fourth-quarter throw against the 49ers. The quarterback amassed a hard-earned 316 yards and two touchdowns, needing 58 attempts to generate 32 completions. (N.Y. Post: Charles Wenzelberg)

special-teams play. Steve Weatherford's punt sailed to Kyle Williams, who was handling all the return duties because Ted Ginn Jr. (knee) was injured and not in uniform.

Williams caught the ball in stride but as he got motoring, rookie linebacker Jacquian Williams reached out with his right arm and poked the ball loose. Devin Thomas, the gunner, alertly pounced on it on the 49ers' 24-yard line, fulfilling Coughlin's hunch that "I felt someone that did not necessarily get the kudos, not someone everyone was familiar with ... I felt someone like that would step up and make the big play."

From there, the Giants knew exactly what to do. They ran Ahmad Bradshaw three times, Manning centered the ball and Tynes lined up for a 26-yard field goal. The Giants were called for a delay-of-game penalty, pushing Tynes back five yards.

"I knew before I picked my head up that it was good," Tynes said.

This was an inelegant, defensive battle filled with stops and sacks and filled with 22 punts, an endurance test that went the distance, and beyond.

The 49ers took a 7-0 lead on a 73-yard touchdown connection from Alex Smith to Vernon Davis, but Manning's six-yard scoring pass to Bear Pascoe and Tynes' 31-yard field goal put the Giants ahead 10-7 at halftime.

Another strike to Davis made it a 14-10 Niners lead in the third quarter, but the Giants got a break early in the fourth quarter when a Steve Weatherford punt glanced off the knee

Above: Ahmad Bradshaw and the Giants' bucks found the going tough on the ground, but No. 44 contributed an important 74 yards on 20 carries. Opposite: Mario Manningham's leaping grab of a 17-yard pass gave the Giants a temporary 17-14 lead midway through the fourth quarter. (N.Y. Post: Charles Wenzelberg)

of Williams, allowing Thomas to recover on the 49ers' 29. That set up Manning's best throw, on third-and-15, to Mario Manningham for a 17-yard strike to put the Giants up 17-14 with 8:34 left in regulation. The Giants couldn't hold the lead and David Akers' 25-yard field goal with 5:39 remaining in the fourth quarter tied it at 17.

Manning, forced to throw 58 times, was sacked six times and afterward had welts on the right side of his face.

"I kept telling myself, 'Be patient, don't give 'em anything,'" said Manning, who listened to his own advice.

The Giants did not have any turnovers on a night when rain, at times heavy, at times misting, made ball security a challenge.

A late drive at the end of regulation died near midfield. The Giants got the ball twice in overtime and couldn't do a darn thing with it. The Giants' defense was just as swarming, limiting Smith's very conservative passing attack.

One team had to blink, and the turnover by Williams was that blink.

Once again, 2007 is reappearing for the Giants.

"Hopefully we will have the same result," Umenyiora said. "We still have one more game to go. But this is truly unbelievable."

Above: Eli Manning is unhurried during this first-quarter pass, but the 49ers defense was punishing throughout the game, sacking him six times. Opposite: Osi Umenyiora (72) and Jason Pierre-Paul (90) were just as tough on San Francisco quarterback Alex Smith. (N.Y. Post: Charles Wenzelberg)

GIANTS ROOKIE THE MOTHER OF ALL HEROES

BY GEORGE WILLIS

It was only a few years ago that Jacquian Williams was ready to give up football. He decided he wasn't going to get back on the airplane and return to Fort Scott Community College. He was ready to give up on the sport.

But his mother, Theolanda, provided a voice of reason.

"She begged me to go back," Williams said last night. "She made me go. I love her for it and I thank her for it. If not for her, I wouldn't be here right now."

Where Williams, Big Blue's rookie linebacker, stood was in a jubilant Giants locker room celebrating a classic 20-17 overtime victory over the 49ers to win the NFC Championship and a berth in Super Bowl XLVI in Indianapolis against the Patriots.

Lawrence Tynes kicked a 31-yard field goal with 7:06 left in overtime to secure the victory. But it was a heads-up, punt-coverage play by Williams that provided the Giants opportunity to kick the game-winner. It also fulfilled a pregame premonition by head coach Tom Coughlin.

Figuring the game on a wet track between two stout defensive teams would be a close, rugged contest, Coughlin's gut told him someone least expected might come up with the game's biggest play.

"I felt like someone who did not necessarily get the kudos and wasn't someone that everyone is familiar with as a guy that's a difference-maker in the game, I thought someone like that would step up and make a big play," the coach said.

That someone proved to be Williams. It came when the Giants' second offensive possession of overtime ended with them punting from their own 44. There was nothing unusual about Steve Weatherford's 37 boot through a light rain. It landed in the hands of 49ers return man Kyle Williams, who was replacing the injured Ted Ginn Jr.

Williams caught the ball cleanly, but just as he tried to make a move Jacquian Williams was there to attempt that tackle.

Williams takes it from there: "I was definitely thinking about going down there and making a play," he said. "I knew somebody had to make it, so I felt like it was going to be me.

"My goal is to make every tackle. So I was going for the tackle. But he made a move and I just stuck my hand at the ball. I saw the ball falling. But I thought he was already done. Obviously he wasn't."

Devin Thomas recovered the fumble for the Giants at the 49ers' 24. Five plays later, Tynes kicked the Giants to Indianapolis and Jacquian Williams, a sixth-round draft pick from South Florida, was Coughlin's unlikely hero.

"There's always somebody who jumps out of the shadows," said Giants GM Jerry Reese.

Williams, 6-foot-3 with a chiseled 225-pound frame, is projected as a future outside linebacker. He saw sporadic duty throughout the season but showed the inconsistency of a rookie. But he continued to work hard throughout the season and impressed coaches with his dedication on special teams.

"It definitely has been a long journey," he said. "It was a lot of battling. We had guys going down and the rookies had to step up and I had to be one of the guys to step up. Rookies don't usually play. But I got the opportunity and I'm glad I did all the fighting and scratching. I just had to be patient."

Of course, none of it happens if his mother hadn't put him back on that plane to finish junior college. She was waiting outside the Giants locker room along with the other players' family members. Mother and son embraced.

"It's something I've dreamed of," Williams said. "To have the opportunity to make a big play in a big game like this."

He has his mom to thank for that. ∎

The play that sent the Giants to Super Bowl XLVI: Devin Thomas pounces on a loose football in overtime—a fumble created when rookie Jaquian Williams (57) stripped the ball from 49ers punt returner Kyle Williams. (N.Y. Post: Charles Wenzelberg)